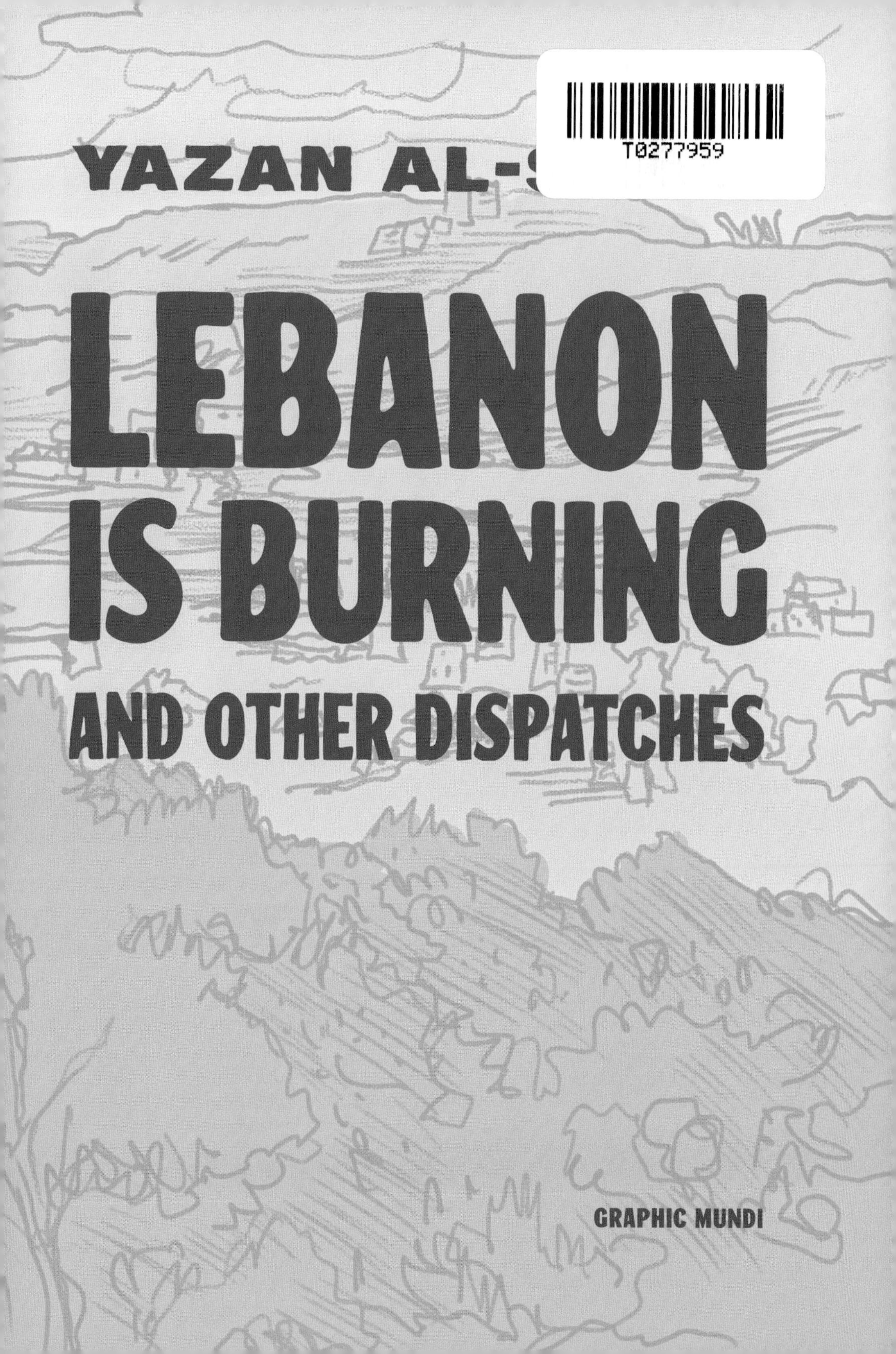

YAZAN AL-S

LEBANON IS BURNING

AND OTHER DISPATCHES

GRAPHIC MUNDI

Cataloging-in-publication data is on file with the Library
of Congress.

The comics from chapters 1, 2, 3, 4, 6, 8, 9, 10, 11, 12, 13, and
14 were originally published by The Nib.

The comic from chapter 5 was originally published in *linus*
magazine.

The comic from chapter 7 was originally published in the
journal *Upping the Anti*. In this comic, the poem "Caged
Bird" from *Shaker, Why Don't You Sing?* by Maya Angelou
is copyright © 1983 by Caged Bird Legacy, LLC, and used
by permission of Random House, an imprint and division
of Penguin Random House LLC. All rights reserved. The
poem "Caged Bird" from *The Complete Collected Poems of
Maya Angelou* is copyright © 1994 by Maya Angelou. Repro-
duced with permission of the Little Brown Book Group
Limited through PLSclear.

Copyright © 2024 Yazan Al-Saadi and Artists
All rights reserved
Printed in China
Published by
The Pennsylvania State University Press,
University Park, PA 16802–1003

10 9 8 7 6 5 4 3 2 1

graphic mundi
drawing our worlds together

Graphic Mundi is an imprint of The Pennsylvania State
University Press.

The Pennsylvania State University Press is a member of the
Association of University Presses.

It is the policy of The Pennsylvania State University Press
to use acid-free paper. Publications on uncoated stock
satisfy the minimum requirements of American National
Standard for Information Sciences—Permanence of Paper
for Printed Library Material, ANSI Z39.48–1992.

CONTENTS

ACKNOWLEDGMENTS

Like a comic book, I was shaped and guided by many hands. If I were to thank them all, I fear I would still be writing these acknowledgments until I vanish from the face of this earth. I owe all of them in one way or another so much for making me the person I am today.

But I'll at least acknowledge the notable few who immediately come to mind.

First and foremost: my parents, Louai and Wafaa, who raised me to be smart, open-minded, and have a huge heart when facing the trials and tribulations of life; my big sister, Dina, who taught me strength and tirelessly challenged me to be better and leap at opportunities; and my wife, Sasha, a source of love and refuge during the most strange and savage days.

Next, I would like to stress my bottomless thanks to all the artists that I had the privilege to work with in making these comics: Enas Satir, Ganzeer, Ghadi Ghosn, Hicham Rahma, Omar Khouri, Sirène Moukheiber, and Tracy Chahwan. Every single one of them deserves accolades and their names firmly etched into stone so future generations know of them and their work until the heat death of the universe. I thank the fates that I cannot draw.

I would be amiss if I didn't say a word or two about The Nib, and in particular Andy Warner, who was my editor and shepherd into the delicate ways of writing a comic script. They have given me a gift and made a lowly comic fan's dream come true and taught me things that I shall never forget.

In the same spirit, I offer gratitude to Anjali Singh, an exceptional and patient agent and supporter of mine for so many years, not to mention one of the coolest persons you can sit down and talk to. Also, I gleefully would like to acknowledge Kendra Boileau, editor for this book, who passionately embraced the collection. Her wise and sensitive edits just made my work better, and she proves the axiom that a writer is absolutely nothing without a damn good editor.

I would especially like to offer undying gratitude to a friend whom I view as a mentor, Fadi Baki. Fadi is the one who pushed me to write comics and his vital, critical eye is a pillar of knowledge and keeps me in line. He is one of the godfathers of the current age of comics in the Arab world; we all owe him much, and anyone interested in the current history of comics in the Arab world must know his name.

Then, there are the countless brave people in the region who resisted, and some continue to resist in spite of the horrific odds. From Palestine to Yemen, Syria to Bahrain, Egypt to Morocco, and beyond. The struggle is never, ever truly over.

And finally, I must mention my two cats—Pampa and Shams—whose cuddles and purring preserved my sanity.

May all the genociders, dictators, and their supporters be smashed by the arc of justice and we collectively build a loving world of liberty and dignity, which every single soul absolutely deserves.

PROLOGUE

This collection of comics arises from the collaboration of numerous talented artists and myself, a Syrian-Canadian journalist, soon to be forty years old, who has toiled for more than a decade as an editor, researcher, communications and creative content manager for Doctors Without Borders—and as a comic strip writer in the callous and alluring city of Beirut, Lebanon. Our collective subjective perspective on events since the 2011 uprisings in the Middle East and North Africa attempts to capture moments within a period of time—perhaps even an underlying zeitgeist—in relation to a geographic area in which I am rooted and where I have lived much of my life. I'm talking about the "West Asian and North African" region, or as it's dubbed in certain places, the "Middle East." But what is "west," "north," "east," or "middle" when you take the long perspective on where we find ourselves—on a ball of rock, spinning along in the vast, dark vacuum of space?

At first glance, I suppose, the view of my region is horrific: disasters, destruction, destitution, dispossession, disarray. Ruthless strongmen, absolute dynasties, ferocious fanatics, brutal bureaucrats, genocidal nation-states, all birthed by infinitely perpetuated, competing, and/or intertwined ideologies and interests. A sprawling stretch of varied landscapes, both blessed *and* cursed by their resources and significant potential, pockmarked by greed and dashed dreams. The coming century opens up before us like an abyss; that light at the end of the tunnel may well be the flash of calamity.

Yet, if we look deeper, we might see a glimmer of hope, a spark of spiteful defiance in this struggle against momentous odds to make things better here, or simply to exist and live. If we look deeper, we discover stories about the human condition and the never-ending drive to persevere.

Affirming perspectives about this place have largely been ignored, caricatured, and/or distorted to suit the whims of authority. But we can see that this region remains vibrant in spite of current and past events, providing an endless well of inspiration and revelation. I must constantly remind myself that the future is not set in stone, that the light at the end of the tunnel may very well be the radiance of celebration.

This collection affirms and embraces the manifesto laid out by the "founder of comic journalism," Joe Sacco, in the introduction of his 2013 collected work *Journalism.* He wrote, "[T]he blessing of an inherently interpretive medium like comics is that it hasn't allowed me to lock myself within the confines of traditional journalism. By making it difficult to draw myself out of the scene, it hasn't permitted me to make a virtue of dispassion. For good or for ill, the comics medium is adamant, and it has forced me to make choices. In my view, that is part of the message." Like Sacco, I too have made my choices in my work, and those choices are influenced by an urgency to support the meek and to strike at the powerful. This is a rebuke of the hegemonic philosophy that has tainted much of journalism's spirit: the oppressiveness of "objectivity."

As a professional journalist and a person of color with an Arab background who has worked in the region and has family and friends here and scattered all over the world, I assert that there is no such thing as absolute objectivity. Objectivity is a tool of privilege that, devoid of the essential components of humanity, too often misses the story. Human beings are not inherently objective. Those of us who live and work in this region take journalism very seriously. We know very well the value of freedom of expression and the power that comes from exposing the corrupt. We know the cost. We remember that more than 700 journalists were killed in Syria over the course of twelve years, the vast majority by a tyrannical, ruthless regime backed by states opposed to the so-called enlightened West. And we remember that more than 120 journalists were killed in Palestinian territory over a period of four months (at the time of this writing) by a merciless apartheid state committing a plausible genocide backed, funded, and armed by the same West. In a profession that is low-paid, thankless, and clearly risky—with the threat of death imminent from every angle and frame—how could we not comprehend the foundational tenets of this work?

The traumas—and there are so many—assailing the region at this very moment were inflicted by internal and external mortal hands. History doesn't end with the last sentence of a history book; it permeates and reverberates and goes on. If you take just a minute to consider some of the terrible events that have happened in this part of the world, like Napoleon's war on Egypt in

1798, the United States' Barbary War of 1801, the famine of WWI, colonialism and Zionism, the war on terror and the invasion of Iraq, it is quite clear that we never had a chance to reckon with the toll each of these horrific events inflicted on their communities before being faced with the next one. How does one heal when there is endless salt pouring into an open wound? It is vital to understand that much of what is currently happening in the Middle East arises as a result of a decaying post-WWII order. Dramatic reorientations are occurring within the international arena. As the global stage reforms itself, the region has become one of the epicenters of upheaval. We have reached a precipice at which available ideologies, spectra, ideas, and beliefs fall severely short in serving the needs of the many.

In Lebanon, my home base, we are threatened by the specter of an all-encompassing war. There is already war in the south of the country's border with a nuclear-armed apartheid state. Grandmothers and children have already been burned to death by drone strikes. White phosphorous has burned olive trees. At least four journalists have been deliberately killed by Israel so far. The threat of a more expansive arena of violence looms and may well be inevitable. For now, I am located in the surreal perimeters of a Schrödinger's war. In the face of all of this—and the many other challenges that lie ahead—we need to reconstruct an internationalist progressive political position. We need an ideology that firmly confronts the cold, calculated acceptance of "politics over people," which enables and justifies the most grotesque of crimes by the powerful against the powerless. The dire conditions we are faced with are not easily relegated to "over there" or to "the other" but instead impact every single soul on this planet.

In the comic journalistic reports dispatched in this collection—whether about the links between the carceral system of settler-colonial states like Canada and Israel, or the question of death in the periphery, or the intoxicating hot energy of an uprising erupting in Lebanon, or the subtle existence of dissent in a suffocating post-Sisi coup in Egypt—we get insight into a particular subject in a specific place and time *and also* a reflection of broader forces at work, repeating themselves throughout human time and space. Perhaps to our great fortune, I cannot draw, and so these stories were visually represented by some of the greatest artistic talents from the region. Not only am I absolutely grateful for the opportunity and privilege to craft stories with these amazing men and women, but I also find it apposite to the overall point I am trying to make. The various styles of art one encounters while reading these comic dispatches one after the other reinforce the idea that stories about such a vibrant and multifaceted region cannot and must not be told from just one perspective. They are best told in tales crafted by collaborative hands.

I hope this collection will provoke the reader to seek out more information about the events in question. Challenge me by reading more about these topics; unpack the whys of what we're trying to depict. From where I sit, I see a world—our one and only home—in grave danger. Climate change, economic exploitation, tyranny, and war are playing out all across the globe. While I am forced to be focused on the immediate concerns of the communities situated around me, I cannot escape the loftier questions of where the hell we are all going collectively as the human race. And clearly, as history has proven relentlessly, the answer to the countless and ever-growing calamities we face will not come from the good graces or moral leadership of those above, who are comfortable for now and zealously convinced that they will remain so. No, the struggle for better tomorrows must come from below; that is the burden of the many. In other words, this collection is, above all, a call to action.

YAZAN AL-SAADI

BEIRUT, LEBANON

MARCH 2024

1. LEBANON IS BURNING

Yazan Al-Saadi and Omar Khouri

The uprising in Lebanon that broke out in October 2019 is but one of a series of social upheavals that date back to before the country's notorious civil war from 1975 to 1990, a war that, arguably, continues in many ways. In the decade I've spent in Lebanon, there have been three massive uprisings against the ruling sectarian regime that had been installed by a regional agreement between Saudi Arabia and Syria and backed by the United States and European states.

During the summer of 2019, you could taste the dissent in the air. I had been forewarned by contacts in the banking system that something big lay ahead. Weeks prior to October of that year, the banks suddenly and illegally imposed capital controls and did not allow their depositors to withdraw their money. Here was an economy that both the World Bank and the International Monetary Fund had lauded, for years, as a great example of capitalism at work. It was, in fact, a massive, sophisticated Ponzi scheme that ultimately reduced the value of the Lebanese lira by more than 90 percent and pushed more than 80 percent of the national population toward poverty.

As the Lebanese uprising progressed, cutting across class and sectarian lines, the various political parties closed their ranks. It did not matter whether these parties were aligned with the west, or with Syria, or with whomever; they were all in accord that the greatest threat was posed by "the masses," and they each worked to undermine, repress, or appropriate the uprising for their own interests.

To date, not one of those in power has been held to account for their theft and oppression. There are many reasons why the uprising failed this time, some of which I'll tackle in later pieces in this collection. But for now, things are a mess. As time passes and memories fade, it's crucial that we remember the fateful day that sparked things. Because it will all happen again in the future, in one way or another.

The artist for this comic is the extraordinary Lebanese Omar Khouri, whom I privately call "The Moebius of Lebanon" in reference to the late, great French artist Jean Giraud (or alternatively, perhaps Giraud was the "Khouri of France"?). Khouri can unleash different and complicated art styles in service of the narrative, and he's an artist who does not back away from attempting very experimental and geeky stuff on the page (as long as it makes sense for the narrative). His chameleonlike talent is showcased in three of the comics featured in this collection. We collaborated on these to capture key events in Lebanon from 2019 to 2023.

I was already a personal fan of Khouri's before I met him and we became friends. I admired his work as a cartoonist and the fact that he was one of the founders of Samandal, a comic collective that has published a series of comics anthologies since the early 2000s and that jump-started the current rage for making comics in this region. Working with him on these pieces was truly a dream come true.

What follows are panel-by-panel notes about the details of this comic, for readers who would like some additional context.

Page 4 (top): While working on the script and talking it over with Omar, we thought it would be interesting to attempt a mapping of the first twenty-four hours of the latest uprising in Lebanon. We looked up news stories, videos, and social media posts, among other material, to create something of a timeline and to capture the events of the day. News stories from domestic, regional, and international outlets were shared and discussed publicly. So here, to mark the first hundred days of the 2019 uprising, we begin on the morning of October 17, 2019, when Lebanon woke up to the news of massive, deadly forest fires and to the usual accounts of xenophobia directed toward the Syrian refugee population in Lebanon.

Page 4 (middle): There were protests in Chile at the time, which ultimately led to a change of regime there and the arrival of one of their youngest leaders.

Page 4 (bottom): Turkey had just launched another attack on northwestern Syria directed toward Syrian Kurdish armed groups. A number of civilians were killed, and Turkey, among others, remains an occupier of Syrian territory.

Page 5 (top): The mention of Hong Kong, with Chile, is to make the point that uprisings were literally ubiquitous.

Page 5 (middle): I believe this is an artistic representation of Omar Khouri, himself, at his balcony.

Pages 5–8: The announcement of outrageous new taxes wasn't really the final straw. It's true that it angered people and they went out into the streets. But I believe the confrontation between protesters and the minister of higher education and his armed bodyguards (i.e., thugs) was the final straw. We used videos and time codes to follow the play-by-play of this historic moment.

Page 9 (top): This iconic image of a woman kicking an armed man in the groin shows how the events of the day culminated. I cannot underscore how epic and powerful this scene was and how it basically motivated a large mass of people to go out into the streets and protest for change. This panel also includes a cheeky reference to divine presence, with the time stamp corresponding to the Bible verse Mark 7:34: "Then, looking up to heaven, He sighed, and said to him, 'Ephphatha,' that is, 'Be opened.'" "Ephphatha" cleverly doubles here as a sound effect.

Pages 9–12: This long unbroken sequence is meant to show the extent to which an uprising can shatter our notions of space and time. In this sequence, the framing falls away, and the narrative elements merge into one another in their complexity. Here I think Khouri succeeds in conveying the passion of this uprising in ways I could not have imagined.

DAY 1: THURSDAY, OCTOBER 17TH, 2019. 7:34 AM

— DISMISSED CLAIMS OF MISMANAGEMENT, BLAMING SYRIAN REFUGEES FOR FOREST FIRES THAT ENGULFED LEBANON SINCE SUNDAY, OCTOBER 13.

ALMOST 3,700 ACRES OF FOREST AND TWO LIVES WERE LOST BEFORE FIREFIGHTERS --

THIS FALL, LEBANON LITERALLY BURNT.

IT WAS A YEAR OF DISCONTENT WITHIN A DECADE OF TURMOIL. AT SUMMER'S END, A LONG PROPHESIED FINANCIAL CRISIS AROSE.

PROTESTS IN CHILE CONTINUE...

8:46 AM

300,000 CIVILIANS FLEE TURKISH ATTACKS IN SYRIA...

10:22 AM

LEBANON HAS A BALLOONING PUBLIC DEBT, CURRENTLY EQUAL TO MORE THAN 150% OF ITS GDP. IT IS THE WORLD'S THIRD-HIGHEST RATIO, AND COULD BECOME THE HIGHEST.

US DOLLARS ARE SCARCE AS THE LEBANESE LIRA FACES DEVALUATION, AND THE NEWS WARNED THAT IMPORTS LIKE MEDICINE, FUEL AND WHEAT WERE AT RISK.

THE PUBLIC HAD LONG SUFFERED THROUGH AUSTERITY, SLASHING AND PRIVATIZATION OF SERVICES, REGRESSIVE TAXES, AND NO REAL POLITICAL REPRESENTATION. THE WEALTH INEQUALITY IS STUNNING. LEBANON HAS THE THIRD HIGHEST DEGREE OF WEALTH INEQUALITY WORLDWIDE.

NEW TAXES WERE ANNOUNCED ON TOBACCO, GASOLINE, AND FREE MESSAGING APPS LIKE WHATSAPP, WHICH MANY LEBANESE RELY ON. SALT ON FESTERING WOUNDS.

IN LEBANON, ONE ROOT, AMONG MANY, WAS PLANTED 30 YEARS AGO AT THE END OF THE 15-YEAR-LONG CIVIL WAR, WITH THE INSTITUTION OF A POLITICAL SECTARIAN POWER-SHARING REGIME, OVERSEEN BY THE U.S., SAUDI ARABIA, AND SYRIA.

5

7:02 PM

FROM 1992 ONWARDS, AN AGGRESSIVE NEOLIBERAL ECONOMIC POLICY WAS LAUNCHED BY THEN-PRIME MINISTER RAFIK HARIRI UNDER THE GUISE OF POST-WAR RECONSTRUCTION.

7:18 PM

PUBLIC LANDS, COASTLINES, AND INDUSTRIES WERE PRIVATIZED, FOREIGN INVESTMENT COURTED AND THE LEBANESE LIRA PEGGED TO THE US DOLLAR. FORMER WARLORDS DONNED SUITS AND GORGED THEMSELVES ON THE PROFITS.

FULLY PROTECTED BY THE SECTARIAN ORDER, THE WARLORDS-CUM-POLITICIANS NURTURED THEIR DYNASTIES. THEIR SONS, SONS-IN-LAW, AND OTHER MALE RELATIVES AND FRIENDS ROSE TO BECOME THE ELITE IN BUSINESS AND POLITICS.

7:27 PM

AKRAM CHEHAYEB, MINISTER OF HIGHER EDUCATION

EVEN AS POLITICAL ALLIANCES SHIFTED AND COALESCED OVER LARGER GEOPOLITICAL CONFLICTS BETWEEN REGIONAL AND WORLD POWERS...

7:28 PM

HIS BODY-GUARDS

...ALL THE RIVAL LEBANESE PARTIES, NO MATTER THEIR EXTERNAL BACKERS, ALIGNED WITH THIS NEOLIBERAL PROJECT TO DOMINATE THE LEBANESE PUBLIC.

GET BACK!!

GET BACK!!

7:29 PM

THIS COLLECTIVELY TRAUMATIZED PEOPLE, BATTERED AND BRUISED BY HISTORY,

ratatatata!

ratatatata!

DON'T SHOOT MAN!

STOP!!

DON'T FUCKIN' SHOOT!

7:30 PM

...WAS FORCED TO WATCH THE POWERFUL PROSPER, EVEN AS THEIR OWN LIVELIHOODS DWINDLED.

7

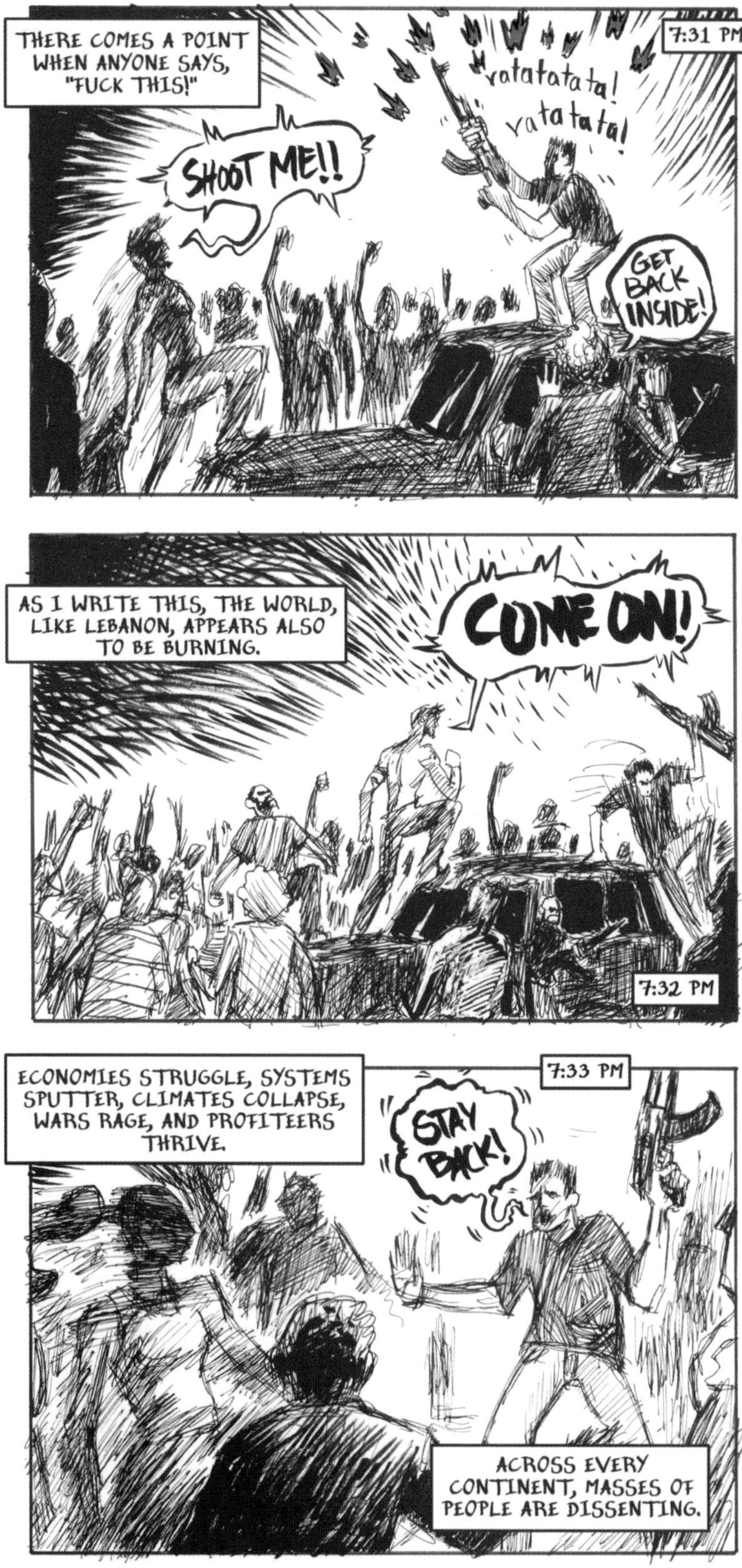
THERE COMES A POINT WHEN ANYONE SAYS, "FUCK THIS!"
7:31 PM
ratatatata!
ratatata!
SHOOT ME!!
GET BACK INSIDE!
AS I WRITE THIS, THE WORLD, LIKE LEBANON, APPEARS ALSO TO BE BURNING.
COME ON!
7:32 PM
ECONOMIES STRUGGLE, SYSTEMS SPUTTER, CLIMATES COLLAPSE, WARS RAGE, AND PROFITEERS THRIVE.
7:33 PM
STAY BACK!
ACROSS EVERY CONTINENT, MASSES OF PEOPLE ARE DISSENTING.

EVERYTHING, AND EVERYONE, HAS A BREAKING POINT.

THAT CLOUDY NIGHT IN LEBANON, TABOOS CRACKED, AND THOUSANDS OF PEOPLE, COMPELLED BY A COLLECTIVE AND RAW RAGE, POURED OUT INTO THE STREETS.

IT WAS A MOMENT OF PURE WONDER AND TERROR THAT STILL REVERBERATE AS TIME LUMBERS ON.

THE SYSTEM GOT SPOOKED. THE NEW PROPOSED TAXES WERE SCRAPPED. A RETREAT TOO LITTLE AND TOO LATE, AS THE PEOPLE BEGAN TO CROSS THE RUBICON.

DAY 3:
2.5 MILLION WENT OUT INTO THE STREETS (36% OF THE POPULATION), THE LARGEST NATIONWIDE PROTEST EVER SEEN. CRUCIALLY, THE PARTICIPANTS CROSSED CLASS, COMMUNITY, AND GEOGRAPHIC LINES, CALLING FOR A JUST INDEPENDENT POLITICAL AND ECONOMIC SYSTEM.

REVOLUTION!

REVOLUTION!

REVOLUTION!

ALL OF THEM MEANS ALL OF THEM

DAY 13: AS PROTESTERS WITHSTOOD INTIMIDATION BY THE ARMY, SECURITY FORCES, AND MILITIA THUGS, PRIME MINISTER SAAD HARIRI RESIGNED, COLLAPSING THE GOVERNMENT. IT WAS A MAJOR VICTORY.

DAY 27: LEBANESE PRESIDENT MICHEL AOUN DECLARED:"IF PEOPLE AREN'T SATISFIED [...] LET THEM EMIGRATE." IN RESPONSE, PROTESTERS ESCALATED CIVIL DISOBEDIENCE TACTICS, BLOCKING ROADS, EXPANDING TENT CAMPS AND CHANTING COLORFUL TAUNTS.

DOWN WITH THE SEXIST SYSTEM, DOWN WITH THE PATRIARCHY!

DAY 18: THUGS LINKED WITH AMAL AND HEZBOLLAH CONDUCT COORDINATED ATTACKS ON PROTEST SITES THROUGHOUT LEBANON, TEARING DOWN TENTS, OR SETTING THEM ON FIRE.

DAY 93: WITH NO GOVERNMENT FORMED, A "WEEK OF WRATH" ANNOUNCED BY PROTESTERS REACHES A CRESCENDO.

TEAR GAS, RUBBER BULLETS, AND THE SECURITY FORCE'S EXCESSIVE BRUTALITY ARE MATCHED BY ROCKS, FIREWORKS, AND INFLAMED ATTACKS AGAINST THE BANKING SECTOR IN THE EVENING.

IMMO... HELA HELA HELA HELA HO! GEBRAN BAS... IMM

DAY 60: THE POWERS-THAT-BE SETTLED IN TO WAIT IT OUT, ANNOUNCING PLANS TO "REFORM" THE SAME GOVERNMENT THAT RESIGNED, AND HOPING THE UPRISING WILL SUCCUMB TO REPRESSION, INTIMIDATION, CO-OPTATION, OR TIME.

DAY 54: PROTESTERS SET UP DEMONSTRATIONS IN FRONT OF THE RESIDENCES OF MINISTERS. A PROTEST CONVOY IS ATTACKED BY INTERNAL SECURITY FORCES, WHO SMASH WINDSHIELDS AND BEAT PEOPLE IN THEIR CARS.

... LET THEM EMIGRATE!

DAY 97: P.M. HASSAN DIAB FORMS A NEW "EXPERT" GOVERNMENT, BUT PROTESTERS ARE UNSATISFIED WITH ITS THINLY VEILED POLITICAL AFFILIATIONS.

AT LEAST 7 HAVE DIED WITH OVER 800 INJURED SINCE OCTOBER 17. THE FUTURE IS OBSCURED WHILE THE PRESENT IS AFLAME.

AND A QUESTION WHISPERS IN EVERYONE'S MIND: WHOSE HANDS WILL PLANT SEEDS AMONG THE ASHES, AND WHAT, IF ANYTHING, WILL GROW?

2.
(IN) HUMANITARIAN WORKERS

Yazan Al-Saadi and Hicham Rahma

I have a complicated relationship with international (i.e., Western) humanitarian organizations, given the shortcomings I perceive in their operations in the Global South, particularly in my region. Often, their work here is irrelevant. At worst, it serves as one of the many barriers to social justice and liberation.

From 2015 to 2019, I worked for Doctors Without Borders (MSF) in the communications department of its emerging branch office in Beirut. I visited MSF projects in Greece, Lebanon, Egypt, Iraq, and Yemen, where I had the privilege of meeting with some incredible human beings—MSF staff and patients—to speak with them about their struggle to survive in the most brutal of circumstances. MSF is a massive operation composed of five operational centers in Europe, each with its respective branch offices around the world. MSF has a budget of over 1.8 billion dollars and operates in more than seventy countries worldwide, where it tackles medical emergencies related to conflict, pandemics, natural disasters, and lack of access to healthcare. It works where few other international organizations dare to go.

But MSF—as progressive as it may be within its sector—is not insulated from biases, ideologies, positions, politics, or history, or the prevalence of sexual harassment, labor exploitation, institutional racism, and manifestations of unacceptable behavior. It is quasi-colonial in structure, and it has, perhaps, one of the worst records on labor rights. Discrimination based on race, gender, sexual preference, and culture is rampant. Those inherent structural biases are intrinsically linked to how the medical organization has grown since its founding in 1971 by a group of French doctors and journalists. The history of MSF is rooted in European colonialism, shaped by post-WWII considerations and Cold War tussles, and its efforts are currently dictated by hegemonic, Western-centric conceptions of "humanitarian values" and appropriate scopes of action. The fuel that allows MSF to function is the seventy thousand workers, medical and nonmedical, of whom over 90 percent are "national staff" (i.e., people hired by MSF to work in offices or on projects within that country). The rest are "expats," often dispatched for senior positions on a temporary basis to oversee the projects. This distinction has created a two-tier system—to the advantage of the expats.

In 2020, inspired by the Black Lives Matter movement in the United States, MSF workers organized to challenge the leadership and demanded radical change. An open letter (https://decolonisemsf.onuniverse.com/2020-open -letter) signed by more than one thousand staff members—unprecedented numbers in the history of MSF—noted the organization's historical failings and its feeble attempts, in recent years, to address these racist structures. The letter asserts their belief that "[e]xclusion, marginalisation and violence are inextricably linked to racism, colonialism and white supremacy, which we reinforce in our work." The open letter ends with ten crucial demands, including a radical reimagining of MSF's approach to humanitarian action, which would focus on affected individuals and communities and seek to redress decades of paternalistic control, as well as an independent external review to evaluate MSF's history of colonialism, expressions of neocolonialism, and manifestations of white supremacy in all aspects of its work. This letter marks a watershed moment for MSF, and since then, a movement has grown within the organization to align its ideologies and actions more with the intersectional concerns of race and labor rights.

The artist I collaborated with is the wonderful Hicham Rahma. I met Hicham during a short residency in Angoulême, France, in the spring of 2022. His caricaturish style really suits the agitating spirit of this comic. The way he represents facial expressions, with cartoony eyes, is simply hilarious.

Page 16 (middle left): The idea to script this comic as a quasi-recruitment video is a response to how hard it has been for MSF to recruit applicants from Lebanon. It's not that people in this region lack interest or expertise. Rather, the problem is that the system doesn't adequately address the needs of workers from the Global South. Case in point: the difficulty of scoring a visa for someone who doesn't hold a powerful passport.

Page 16 (middle/bottom): Many of these talking points are taken directly from what MSF and other international humanitarian organizations use to brand and market themselves to the public. It's become so corporate and devoid of meaning at this point.

Page 17 (top left): These are typical upper-management talking points, whether from corporate entities like Apple or humanitarian organizations like MSF.

Page 17 (bottom): The idea of unionizing humanitarian workers is a powerful one. Workers in the NGO sector, especially in the Global South, need this type of representative body to pressure and fight for more equitable terms. We know that these institutions will not change on their own.

(in) Humanitarian WORKERS

BY Yazan Al-saadi HichamRahma

FOUR YEARS WORKING FOR A MEDICAL AID NGO TAUGHT ME THAT HUMANITARIAN WORK IS OFTEN INHUMANE. THE SECTOR IS RIFE WITH LABOR EXPLOITATION, INEQUALITY, STRUCTURAL RACISM AND SEXISM...

BUT FROM THE OUTSIDE, IT'S EASY TO THINK THAT PEOPLE WILL GLADLY TAKE ON MORE BURDEN BECAUSE THEY'RE "HELPING PEOPLE." THIS IMAGE IS ESSENTIAL IN HOW THE HUMANITARIAN SECTOR SELLS ITSELF.

QUIET ON SET! WE'RE FILMING!

RECRUITMENT VIDEO, TAKE 2. ACTION!

YOU WANT TO BE A HUMANITARIAN WORKER? IT'S THE ADVENTURE OF A LIFETIME! NOTHING IS MORE SATISFYING THAN HELPING THE NEEDY!

YOU'LL BE IN BASIC ENVIRONMENTS WITH LOCAL STAFF. PREPARE TO LEAVE BEHIND COMFORTS LIKE SHOWERS AND WIFI; IT'S LIKE CAMPING! YOU'LL MEET QUIRKY CULTURES.

ALWAYS KEEP AN OPEN MIND!

THESE ARE STRESSFUL ENVIRONMENTS. BUT DON'T WORRY: IF THINGS GET UGLY, WE'LL MAKE SURE YOU'RE ON THE NEXT PLANE HOME!

UM... DO WE "NEEDY LOCALS" GET TO LEAVE TOO?

HEY NOW, THEY GOTTA PRIORITIZE!

WHO CAN GUARANTEE VISAS TO THE WEST? NOT THEIR MANDATE!

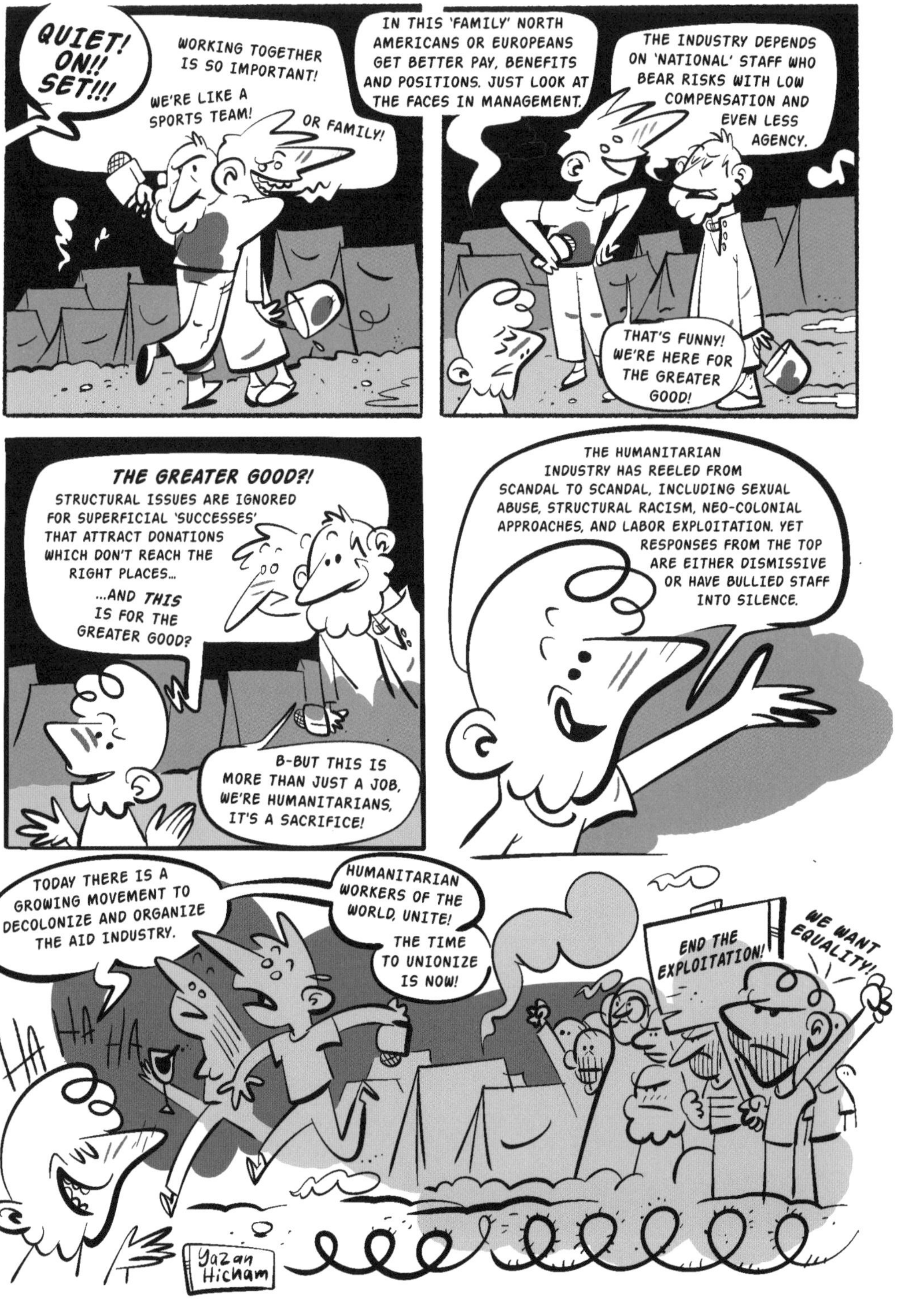
QUIET! ON!! SET!!!
WORKING TOGETHER IS SO IMPORTANT!
WE'RE LIKE A SPORTS TEAM!
OR FAMILY!
IN THIS 'FAMILY' NORTH AMERICANS OR EUROPEANS GET BETTER PAY, BENEFITS AND POSITIONS. JUST LOOK AT THE FACES IN MANAGEMENT.
THE INDUSTRY DEPENDS ON 'NATIONAL' STAFF WHO BEAR RISKS WITH LOW COMPENSATION AND EVEN LESS AGENCY.
THAT'S FUNNY! WE'RE HERE FOR THE GREATER GOOD!
THE GREATER GOOD?! STRUCTURAL ISSUES ARE IGNORED FOR SUPERFICIAL 'SUCCESSES' THAT ATTRACT DONATIONS WHICH DON'T REACH THE RIGHT PLACES... ...AND THIS IS FOR THE GREATER GOOD?
B-BUT THIS IS MORE THAN JUST A JOB, WE'RE HUMANITARIANS, IT'S A SACRIFICE!
THE HUMANITARIAN INDUSTRY HAS REELED FROM SCANDAL TO SCANDAL, INCLUDING SEXUAL ABUSE, STRUCTURAL RACISM, NEO-COLONIAL APPROACHES, AND LABOR EXPLOITATION. YET RESPONSES FROM THE TOP ARE EITHER DISMISSIVE OR HAVE BULLIED STAFF INTO SILENCE.
TODAY THERE IS A GROWING MOVEMENT TO DECOLONIZE AND ORGANIZE THE AID INDUSTRY.
HUMANITARIAN WORKERS OF THE WORLD, UNITE!
THE TIME TO UNIONIZE IS NOW!
HA HA HA
END THE EXPLOITATION!
WE WANT EQUALITY!
Yazan Hicham

3.
BAHRAIN'S INCONVENIENT REVOLUTION

Yazan Al-Saadi and Ghadi Ghosn

At one point during the uprisings in 2011 in Bahrain, a country with a total population of 1.212 million, more than 300,000 people flooded the streets. They demanded liberty and dignity in the face of an absolute monarch who was backed by regional Arab Gulf states and the West, especially the United States during the Obama administration. This figure—300,000—is according to the Bahrain Center for Human Rights, although the regime says it was more like 100,000. Even if we split the difference, that's still more protesters, per capita, than in the protests that followed the death of George Floyd in the United States.

During these protests in Bahrain, more than 180 protesters were killed and 17 security officers died; more than 3,000 people were wounded; 3,000 were arrested; 1,500 were exiled; and 900 were stripped of their citizenship.

The history of Bahrain is fascinating and often obscure. Much of the Arab Gulf has been understudied, particularly from the point of view of social mobilization and the potential for radical political change. Bahrain has a lot of potential for radical change, and this is perhaps why the neighboring regimes, with blessings from the West, managed to annihilate much of the Bahraini uprising within just weeks.

I see many parallels between Syria and Bahrain. Both are controlled by young men who rose to power proclaiming promises of reward. In reality, these leaders head absolute dynasties that benefit a minority over a majority and that are backed by external powers. Both countries are rich in history and caught in waves of fate. It is no wonder, then, that the ruling regimes of Syria and Bahrain, in spite of ideological differences, supported one other during a time of counterrevolution. Syrians and Bahrainis are bound together in more ways than they often realize.

When I wrote this comic, Donald Trump was president of the United States and had deepened US support for the ruler of Bahrain, Hamad bin Isa bin Salman Al Khalifa, and his repression of the populace that began even as early as Barack Obama's presidency. President Joe Biden continues that support, underlining once again for communities in the Middle East that the Democrats and the Republicans don't differ much when it comes to US foreign policy in the region.

This comic was drawn by Ghadi Ghosn, a Lebanese artist who has become my go-to collaborator time and time again for both nonfiction and fiction comics. He is a marvelous artist and human being.

Pages 21–22: This comic demonstrates the weaponization of history.

Page 23 (top right): With his masterful use of perspective, Ghadi succeeds here in transforming my vague suggestion for showing the area's history of imperial domination with this monstrous image of a human chain of invaders trouncing the region.

Pages 23 (bottom) and 24: Again, Ghadi experiments with spatial interpretation to represent the ever-changing imperial patrons that have dominated Bahrain.

Pages 25 (bottom) and 26 (top left): The pink building in the background of this protest scene and line of bulldozers references the Pearl Monument and roundabout, which was the site of the camp set up by the protesters. The Bahrain and the Gulf Cooperation Council (GCC) forces ultimately demolished the Pearl Monument and scrubbed its likeness from the currency and other official sites. This site is now called the Al-Farooq Junction and has been replaced by traffic lights.

Page 26 (bottom right): Maryam Al-Khawaja is a phenomenal human being and a tireless advocate for her community and its quest for self-determination. She is the daughter of the prominent human rights defender Abdulhadi Al-Khawaja, who has been a political prisoner of the state for over a decade and suffers now from dire health issues.

Page 27 (top right): The Bahrain Independent Commission of Inquiry (BICI) was established in June 2011 by the state to "investigate" any abuses by security forces during the uprising. It was a strategy to deflect domestic and international critique in the aftermath of the crackdown. When the government established the committee, criticism from Western states and international institutions diminished. Despite the arguably tame recommendations in the committee's five-hundred-page report, which was released in November 2011, the regime did not fully implement any actions for accountability or justice regarding human rights abuses.

Page 27 (bottom left): This image is based on a photo taken on May 21, 2017, at a meeting between Trump and Al Khalifa that marked a new repressive and bloody turn. Since then, Bahrainis have continued to protest, inspired by other events in the region, especially in Palestine. The normalized relationship between Bahrain and Israel by way of the Abraham Accords is not supported by the public. As a result, protests have erupted over the years and have intensified. Even before the Abraham Accords, the Al Khalifa regime and Israel were linked by shared interests in opposing Iran.

Page 27 (bottom right): Maryam makes a beautiful concluding point here, one with which I wholeheartedly agree.

"Bahrain" is Arabic for "two seas."

A fitting name. The body of water it sits in is subject to dispute—whether it's the Persian Gulf or Arabian Gulf depends on who you ask. Two names for two seas.

Names are one thing. History is another.

And in Bahrain, looking too far back in time can get you in trouble.

From far away Bahrain seems miniscule, quirky, harmless, rich.

A cluster of islands in the Gulf. Qatar to its east. Saudi Arabia to its west. Iran's shoreline far across the water.

295.5 square miles in size, population 1.5 million (800,000 are nationals).

Ruled by the Al Khalifa family since 1783. Home to the naval base of the US Fifth Fleet, lynchpin of the US wars in Iraq and Afghanistan.

Since 2011, it has been rocked by revolution and crushed by counterrevolution.

Syria

Iraq

Iran

Jordan

Kuwait

BAHRAIN

Qatar

United Arab Emirates

Saudi Arabia

Oman

I worked as a journalist during the 2011 uprisings. While having a drink in Beirut, Lebanon, a friend told me a story that took place in Bahrain, where she worked.

She was teaching history in Manama, the capital.

...after Bahrain's ruling al-Khalifa family came from Zubara (Qatar) and conquered Bahrain in the early 1780s...

(A factual statement.)

The Next Day.

A student from a powerful family complained.

If you ever mention Al Khalifa being from Qatar again, you're out.

The ruling Al-Khalifa is adamant that they are eternal. They are Bahrain.

Bahrain is them.

Do you understand?

But Bahrain's story has more depth.

The country's strategic location along the shores of the Arabian Peninsula has long been precarious for its people.

The islands saw domination after domination. Babylon, Persia, Alexander the Great, Islam, the Portuguese, the Safavids and finally, in 1783, "Ahmad the Conqueror."

Backed by a fleet from Kuwait, an army of several clans and tribes, Ahmad ibn Muhammed ibn Khalifa seized Bahrain and established a dynasty that has ruled ever since.

In the early 1800s, the Al Khalifa turned to the British to shore up their rule against regional rivals.

The British recognized the dominance of Al Khalifa and handled their security. When petroleum was later discovered, the British profited massively.

The baton of empire was passed to the US during WWII, although the British 'officially left' in 1971.

The Americans maintained Al Khalifa's control, and based their largest naval presence in the Middle East in Bahrain's waters.

Bahrain's people never remained silent about Al Khalifa's absolute, autocratic rule.

As far back as the 1920s, Bahrainis launched one of the oldest civil rights movements and the first leftist political party in the Gulf region. Almost like clockwork, uprisings flared up every few decades.

Representation is at the heart of the struggle.

Al Khalifa is Sunni, while the majority of Bahrainis are Shia. Yet it's not just about sect, which Al Khalifa did exploit to divide-and-rule.

There's also monopolization of resources and land rights by the ruling family, on top of Bahraini society's marginalization along political, economic and social levels.

Abuses like collective punishment, murder, exile, large-scale incarcerations, and torture fuel dissent.

Inspired by uprisings in the region, the Bahrainis mobilized once again in February 2011.

At one point, more than 300,000 Bahrainis — from different sects and backgrounds — flooded the streets. Roughly, 43 percent of the national population.

Akin to 140 million American citizens protesting simultaneously.

25

Al Khalifa's security forces clamped down swiftly, backed by the Peninsula Shield regional army of the Saudi-dominated Gulf Coordination Council (GCC).

Protest spaces were bulldozed, emergency care for protesters was criminalized and NGOs like Doctors Without Borders were ousted from the country. Thousands were incarcerated, thus Bahrain has one of, if not the highest prison population rates in the region.

The uprising was tarred as an "Iranian and Qatari conspiracy" and ignored.

In 2014, from Beirut, I spoke over the phone with Nabeel Rajab, a prominent opposition leader and human rights activist, about these challenges.

Even the Syrian regime supported the Peninsula Shield's invasion of Bahrain. Repressive regimes work together while we are still finding it difficult being allies. Solidarity... It is our only hope!

Not long after, Rajab was arrested in October 2014. He was released in July 2015, arrested once more in June 2016, and earlier in 2018 sentenced for criticizing the Saudi war on Yemen and "disseminating false news, statements and rumours about the internal situation of the kingdom that would undermine its prestige and status."

Maryam Al-Khawaja, Bahraini-Danish human rights activist. She has been jailed, lives in exile and faces an arrest warrant and a handful of pending cases. Her father, a human rights activist leader, is currently in prison for life and has been tortured.

She, perhaps, articulates it best.

When I'm asked to describe the revolution to audiences, especially Western audiences, I resort to calling Bahrain an "inconvenient revolution."

It's inconvenient to the West, the US, Europe. It's inconvenient to the GCC and other Arab regimes, while Iran uses Bahrain as a bargaining chip. There are reasons why coverage on Bahrain is limited.

And Al Khalifa manipulates discourse and mechanisms of international human rights accountability to buy more time. The West simply says, 'Oh, the Bahraini government has promised to reform, promised to stop abuses, promised accountability, give them time.'

The Bahrain Independent Commission of Inquiry (BICI)

But things are getting worse.

Trump's meeting the Bahraini king in May 2017 gave the green light for more repression. Two days later, Bahraini security forces attacked a peaceful sit-in, killing five people, injuring more than 100, and arresting almost 300 people. This is the deadliest attack in years.

What they don't realize...Bahrainis will continue to protest. It's not going to stop. Not at all. Not until they get their rights.

27

4.
EIGHT YEARS OF UNREST IN SYRIA

Yazan Al-Saadi and Omar Khouri

This comic marks the eighth anniversary of the outbreak of an uprising-turned-civil/proxy war in Syria. Yes, I know that's a strange description for what happened and continues to happen in Syria. Is there a more suitable shorthand to describe the events in a country experiencing an uprising with revolutionary potential against a brutal totalitarian dynastic regime, which transformed into a quasi–civil war with sectarian trappings between asymmetrical armed groups, each backed by various competing regional and international powers that also, for their part, got directly involved in the fighting or are occupying parts of the country? I suppose the grim circumstances excuse a run-on sentence. But calling it grim is also an understatement.

When I wrote the script for this comic, I was grappling with paralysis in terms of what to write about the tragedy in Syria that hadn't already been said. The problem was not in the telling but in being heard. This was pretty much the situation from all points of view, where talking about Syria was only divisive and ultimately led to the silencing of Syrian voices, which were then supplanted by the louder voices of those who didn't care about the Syrians and were rather driven by their own ideological positions.

At the time, the most salient narrative was that "Assad had won" and that it was time to normalize—despite the fact that the guns were not yet silent and the core issues causing the uprising were not yet resolved. Moreover, the parts of the country that hadn't been bombed by four out of the five United Nations Security Council members (as well as the Assad regime and the armed opposition) were occupied by Russian, Iranian, Israeli, and Turkish armed forces.

The point of this comic was to tackle that axiom of Assad's victory, and my partner in this endeavor was Omar Khouri, whose exceptional, steady hand created a matter-of-fact comic that wrestled with the political and philosophical aspects of the Syrian uprising. We wanted to be as factual as possible, given all the misinformation that was circulating. The facts are undeniable: Syria is a dictatorship; much of the armed opposition came from sectarian and religious fundamentalist groups; there was foreign intervention; the Assad regime used chemical weapons on the population; there was rampant torture and sexual violence; and neither the regime nor the opposition really cared about the welfare of the Syrian people.

Page 31: This is our attempt to riff on the iconic image from the infamous Japanese manga *Akira* by Katsuhiro Otomo.

Page 32: As I write this, we're looking at half a million dead and almost one million suffering from disabilities and physical/mental difficulties. Millions remain displaced, and their homes have not been rebuilt.

Page 33 (top): The hospital, Dar al-Shifa, that Omar reproduces here was in Aleppo. Attacks on hospitals, medical centers, doctors, nurses, ambulances, and other vital civilian infrastructure were part and parcel of the war strategy by the Assad regime and its allies. Of course, this kind of thing is not exclusive to Syria. Attacks on hospitals are a common and barbaric war tactic used by the United States and its allies as well as by Russia and its allies. Additionally, we've seen this in Afghanistan, Iraq, Vietnam, and, of course, in Palestine.

Page 34: The sanctions have not affected the ruling regime, which has continued to profit from the situation while the Syrian populace pays the eternal price.

Page 35 (bottom): This is an artistic depiction of a real photo taken on the outskirts of Aleppo, in northern Syria.

Page 36 (bottom): Another riff on a real photo of the many useless and theatrical meetings that were sponsored by "Friends of Syria" or "Supporting Syria" and so forth. None of these meetings helped Syrians. We need only consider how, for a long time, neither Europe nor the Arab world attempted to open its borders to the refugees.

Page 38: Of the many horrors that occurred in Syria, perhaps the most unifying one, cutting across political and ideological lines, is the disappearance of thousands of citizens into the prison system. The "Caesar photos" played an important role, I believe, in rallying the population against all those who committed such crimes. While these photos were clearly politicized by the West, who cared not at all about disappeared Syrians, it was still important for Syrians themselves to learn what had happened to their loved ones. There is no excuse or justification for this horror.

Page 39 (top): This art is based on aerial photographs of the notorious Sednaya prison. Every Syrian is well aware of Sednaya's shadow.

Page 40 (top): The art here is inspired by a photo of one of the many protests by "Families for Freedom," an organization of Syrian relatives of those who were missing or kidnapped by opposition armed groups. These protests often took place in Europe and were usually ignored by the political elites.

Page 40 (bottom): I think about transformative justice a lot. We need meaningful accountability in Syria in order to have sustainable justice for all. Without this, history will be destined to repeat itself.

IT HAS BEEN EIGHT YEARS SINCE THE SYRIAN UPRISING ERUPTED, AND THE GENERAL CONSENSUS IS THAT BASHAR AL-ASSAD IS VICTORIOUS.

WHAT HAS HE WON?

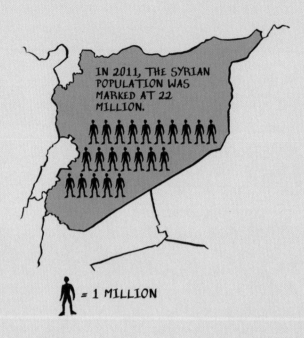

IN 2011, THE SYRIAN POPULATION WAS MARKED AT 22 MILLION.

= 1 MILLION

SINCE THEN,

AN ESTIMATED HALF A MILLION HAVE DIED IN THE CONFLICT.

ALMOST A MILLION MORE SUFFER FROM PHYSICAL AND/OR MENTAL DISABILITIES.

AROUND 12 MILLION ARE EITHER INTERNALLY DISPLACED OR ARE REFUGEES OUTSIDE THE COUNTRY.

LOOKING AT SYRIA TODAY, VARIOUS ESTIMATES PAINT A STARK AND GRIM PICTURE.

BEFORE 2011, SYRIA WAS
A MIDDLE-INCOME
COUNTRY, WITH A
ROBUST HEALTH CARE
SYSTEM.

95% OF THE POPULACE
NOW LACK ACCESS TO
ADEQUATE HEALTH CARE.
MALE LIFE EXPECTANCY
SHRANK FROM 71 YEARS
IN 2011 TO 59 YEARS IN
2018, WHILE IT DROPPED
FROM 71 TO 69 YEARS
FOR WOMEN.

MEDICAL SERVICES IN AREAS BEYOND THE
REGIME'S CONTROL WERE DEEMED TERRORISM.
MANY DIFFERENT SIDES IN THE CONFLICT
TARGETED HOSPITALS AND CLINICS.

MEDICAL WORKERS FLED, AND THE REMAINING
FEW WITNESSED THE MOST BARBARIC DEEDS.

SYRIA'S ECONOMY HAS
COLLAPSED DUE TO
WAR, AND SANCTIONS
IMPOSED BY THE US, EU,
AND OTHER STATES.

THE SANCTIONS WERE JUSTIFIED
TO WEAKEN ASSAD'S REGIME, BUT
THE POPULATION BORE THE BRUNT.

4 IN 5 SYRIANS ARE LIVING IN POVERTY, WITH 30 PERCENT OF THE POPULATION UNABLE TO MEET BASIC HOUSEHOLD FOOD NEEDS.

THE SCORCHED EARTH POLICY OF THE SYRIAN MILITARY AND ALLIED MILITIAS, THE RUSSIAN AND US-LED COALITION AIRSTRIKES, AND INDISCRIMINATE FIRE BY OPPOSITION GROUPS HAVE DESTROYED 1/3 OF HOMES AND LARGE SWATHS OF AGRICULTURAL FIELDS, INDUSTRY, HISTORICAL SITES, AND MORE.

THE UN ECONOMIC AND SOCIAL COMMISSION FOR WESTERN ASIA ESTIMATES THE PRICE TAG OF DESTRUCTION AT MORE THAN $388 BILLION.

MEANWHILE DISASTER CAPITALISM HAS ARRIVED AND POLITICIANS AND BUSINESSES SALIVATE ABOUT SYRIA'S 'RECONSTRUCTION'.

IT'S THE NEW MANTRA OVER THE PAST FEW YEARS, PRESENTED AS 'SUPPORT FOR THE COUNTRY'.

EUROPEAN, RUSSIAN, AND LEBANESE POLITICIANS, DRIVEN BY A DESIRE TO RETURN SYRIAN REFUGEES, HELD CONFERENCES TO FOCUS ON REBUILDING SYRIA, EVEN AS THE WAR(S) ON THE GROUND RAGED ON.

IN THE EAST, PAST THE EUPHRATES RIVER, THE US-BACKED SYRIAN DEMOCRATIC FORCE (SDF), AN ALLIANCE LED BY THE KURDISH PEOPLE'S PROTECTION UNITS, BATTLES ISIS AND PREPARES FOR A POTENTIAL CONFRONTATION WITH THE TURKISH MILITARY IN THE NORTH.

IN THE NORTH-WEST PROVINCE OF IDLIB ARMED OPPOSITION GROUPS - MOSTLY REACTIONARY AND FUNDAMENTALIST - FIGHT EACH OTHER AND TARGET INDEPENDENT SYRIAN ACTIVISTS, EVEN AS ASSAD'S BOMBS STILL FALL ON VILLAGES, TOWNS, AND CITIES.

SYRIA'S VERY SOVEREIGNTY IS IN QUESTION AS TURKISH, IRANIAN, ISRAELI, RUSSIAN, AMERICAN, EUROPEAN, AND OTHER MILITARY FORCES OCCUPY GROUND, ESTABLISH MILITARY BASES, AND ROUTINELY DROP THEIR BOMBS ON A BATTERED, BROKEN NATION.

IN THE REST OF THE COUNTRY — OVER 60%
OF THE LAND — UNDER THE CONTROL OF THE
ASSAD REGIME, ARBITRARY ARRESTS AND
TORTURE INCREASE RELENTLESSLY.

THERE ARE HUNDREDS OF
THOUSANDS WHO HAVE
VANISHED WITHIN THE
REGIME'S PRISONS SINCE
2011, WITH MORE EVERY
DAY.

LAST YEAR, THE REGIME BEGAN
RELEASING 'DEATH NOTICES' FOR
PEOPLE THAT DISAPPEARED INTO
THE PRISONS AS MANY AS SIX
YEARS EARLIER. THE DEATHS
WERE OF "NATURAL CAUSES." NO
BODIES RETURNED, ONLY PAPER.

YET THE INFAMOUS "CAESAR
PHOTOS" — 55,000 IMAGES OF
11,000 DEAD MEN, WOMEN, AND
CHILDREN, SMUGGLED OUT BY
A DEFECTOR IN 2013 —
INDICATE STARVATION,
TORTURE, AND EXECUTIONS.

THEIR VALIDITY HAS BEEN
VERIFIED, INCLUDING BY
RELATIVES OF THE DEAD
WHO RECOGNIZE THEIR
FACES AND BODIES.

IN A 2016 REPORT, UN HUMAN RIGHTS INVESTIGATORS
WROTE OF A WELL-SOURCED SYSTEMATIC "STATE POLICY
OF EXTERMINATION OF THE CIVILIAN POPULATION".

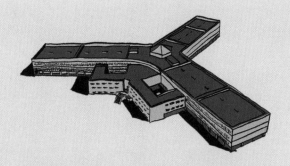

THE ASSAD REGIME WAS ALWAYS NOTORIOUS FOR ITS PRISONS AND TORTURE. LONG BEFORE 2011, WE SYRIANS SHIVERED UNDER THE SEDNAYA PRISON'S SHADOW.

THERE ARE STILL PLENTY WHO REMAIN ALIVE IN THESE PRISONS, AND AS TIME PASSES, MANY MORE COULD PERISH. THIS SOBERING FACT MAKES APPEALS FOR THEIR IMMEDIATE RELEASE URGENT AND DESPERATE.

ORGANIZATIONS LIKE FAMILIES FOR FREEDOM —
ESTABLISHED BY SURVIVORS OF THE DISAPPEARED
(INCLUDING THOSE KIDNAPPED BY ARMED
OPPOSITION GROUPS) — TIRELESSLY ADVOCATE IN
NEGOTIATIONS, CONFERENCES, AND SUMMITS.

SO FAR, THEY'VE BEEN IGNORED BY
DIPLOMATS, DESPITE HOW UNIFYING THEIR
CALL IS FOR SYRIANS OF DIFFERENT
BACKGROUNDS. IT CUTS TO THE HEART, AND
SUGGESTS A LONGER STRUGGLE IN SYRIA.

TRUTH, JUSTICE, AND
ACCOUNTABILITY ARE
ESSENTIAL TO ANY
HEALING OR
SUSTAINABLE PEACE
ONCE THE GUNS FALL
SILENT.

THIS IS A (NEGLECTED) LESSON
THAT ALL CIVIL WARS,
GENOCIDES, AND OTHER HUMAN
HORRORS HAVE REVEALED TIME
AND TIME AGAIN THROUGHOUT
OUR WORLD.

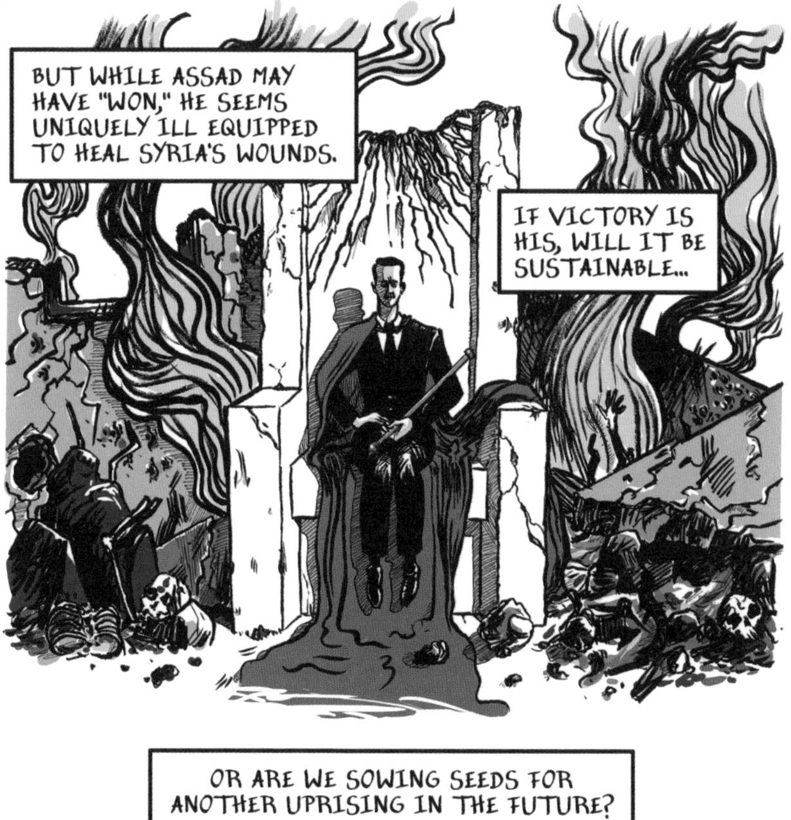
BUT WHILE ASSAD MAY HAVE "WON," HE SEEMS UNIQUELY ILL EQUIPPED TO HEAL SYRIA'S WOUNDS.
IF VICTORY IS HIS, WILL IT BE SUSTAINABLE...
OR ARE WE SOWING SEEDS FOR ANOTHER UPRISING IN THE FUTURE?

5.
Eppur Si Muove

Yazan Al-Saadi and Ghadi Ghosn

Patrick Zaki was an Egyptian student at the University of Bologna. While visiting family in Egypt in February 2020, he was arrested by security forces for spreading fake news and inciting protests. While in detention, he was interrogated about his human rights work, beaten, and tortured.

Zaki was one of a handful of academics who were targeted by the Egyptian state. But his case captured the attention of the Italian public (and broader European audiences) because of his links to the University of Bologna and some perceived parallels between his case and that of the Italian researcher Giulio Regeni, who was tortured to death in Egypt in 2016. Zaki would ultimately be released and pardoned by the Egyptian authorities in July 2023.

I collaborated with Ghadi Ghosn on this comic with the idea of making it as relevant as possible to Italian audiences, which is why we drew out the parallels between Italy's own history of repression and what was happening in Egypt today. The Sisi regime in Egypt is terrifying: Sisi has become the world's third-leading jailer for journalists and others.

Page 44: Galileo's experience is not much different from other people's experiences in the face of repressive systems, be they religious or secular. When Galileo uses the phrase "Eppur si muove" (And yet it still moves), he is, of course, talking about the movements of celestial bodies. Here I reinterpret the phrase to mean that civil disobedience and social uprisings still continue, despite any form of repression.

Page 45: To emphasize the parallels, the composition of the page mirrors that of the previous story of Galileo.

Page 46: This splash page by Ghadi is both beautiful and uncomfortable. How else should one feel when describing torture?

Page 48: We used the soccer analogy here to appeal to an Italian audience. It's important to note that not all Italians are neutral parties when it comes to Egypt, a point I make in the next parts of this comic.

Pages 49–50: Ghadi's art here is inspired by actual photographs taken during meetings with Egyptian officials in Italy and in Europe over the "migrant crisis." For Italy and other European states, it matters little whether they're dealing with authoritarian regimes as long as those regimes are in agreement with the interests of the European Union—meaning, in this case, that they support a barrier between "fortress Europe" and the masses of people desperately searching for a better life there.

Page 51 (middle): "2+2=5" is taken from George Orwell's *1984*. Not much has changed since then in how repressive regimes react to the facts on the ground, especially if these facts threaten to undermine their power structures. But, as is noted time and time again in this comic, dissent will always persist. Always.

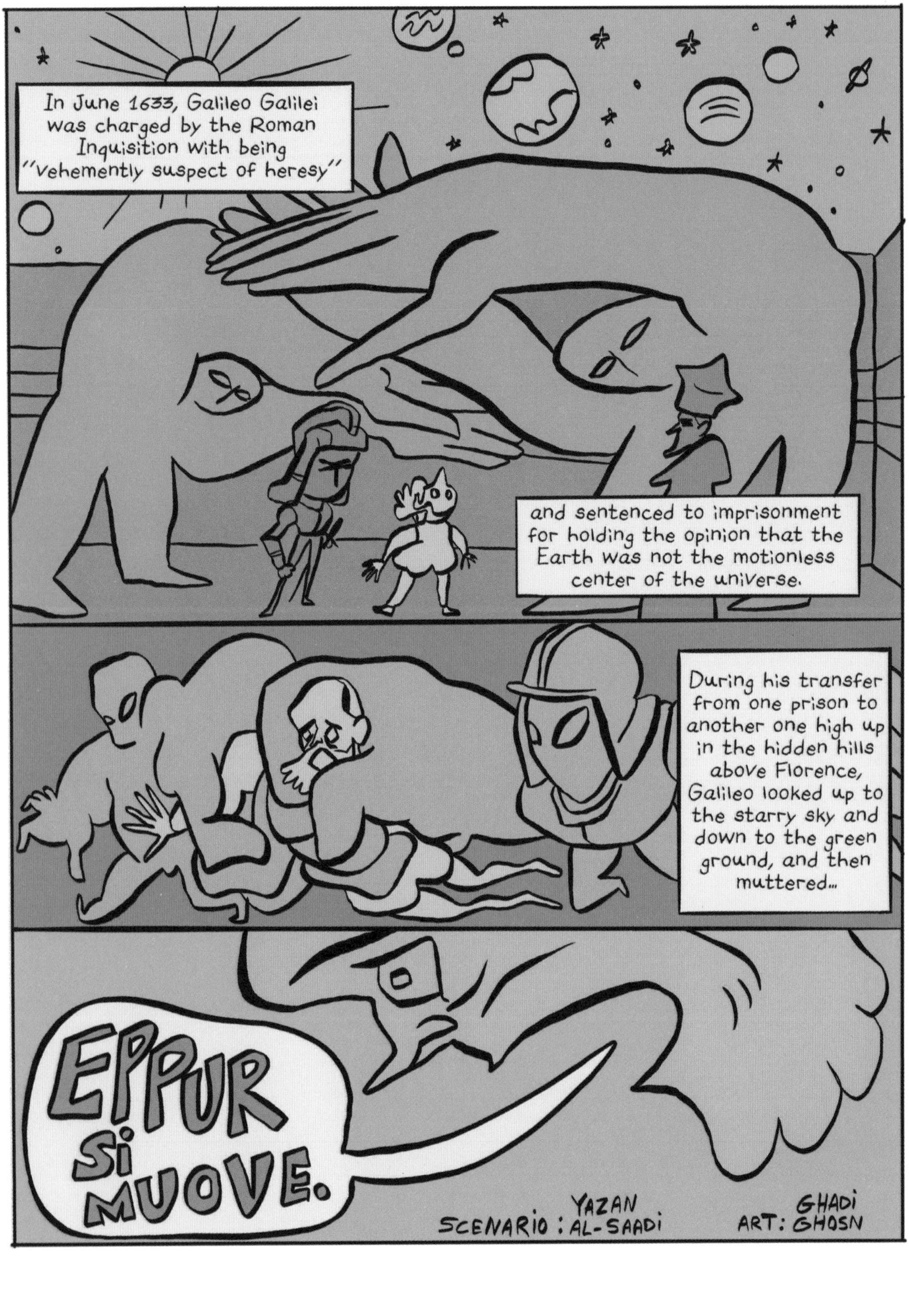
In June 1633, Galileo Galilei was charged by the Roman Inquisition with being "vehemently suspect of heresy"
and sentenced to imprisonment for holding the opinion that the Earth was not the motionless center of the universe.
During his transfer from one prison to another one high up in the hidden hills above Florence, Galileo looked up to the starry sky and down to the green ground, and then muttered...
EPPUR Si MUOVE.
SCENARIO : YAZAN AL-SAADi
ART: GHADi GHOSN

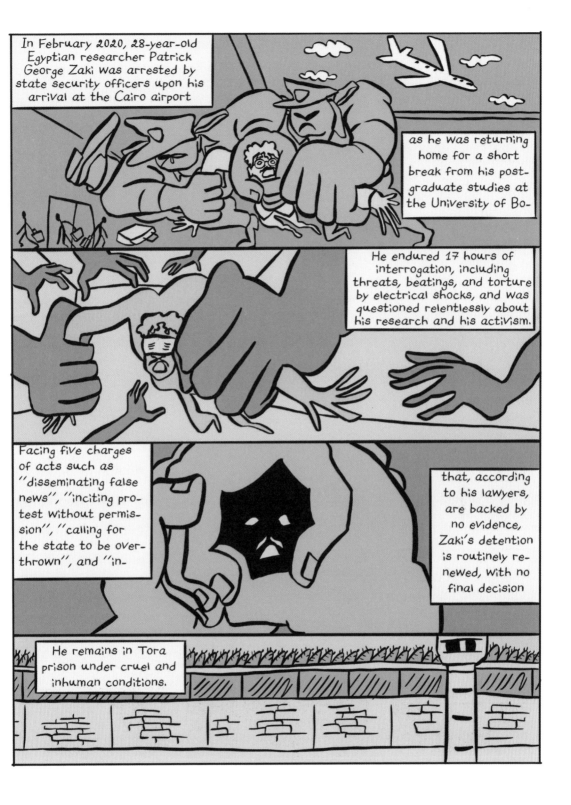

In February 2020, 28-year-old Egyptian researcher Patrick George Zaki was arrested by state security officers upon his arrival at the Cairo airport

as he was returning home for a short break from his post-graduate studies at the University of Bo-

He endured 17 hours of interrogation, including threats, beatings, and torture by electrical shocks, and was questioned relentlessly about his research and his activism.

Facing five charges of acts such as "disseminating false news", "inciting protest without permission", "calling for the state to be overthrown", and "in-

that, according to his lawyers, are backed by no evidence, Zaki's detention is routinely renewed, with no final decision

He remains in Tora prison under cruel and inhuman conditions.

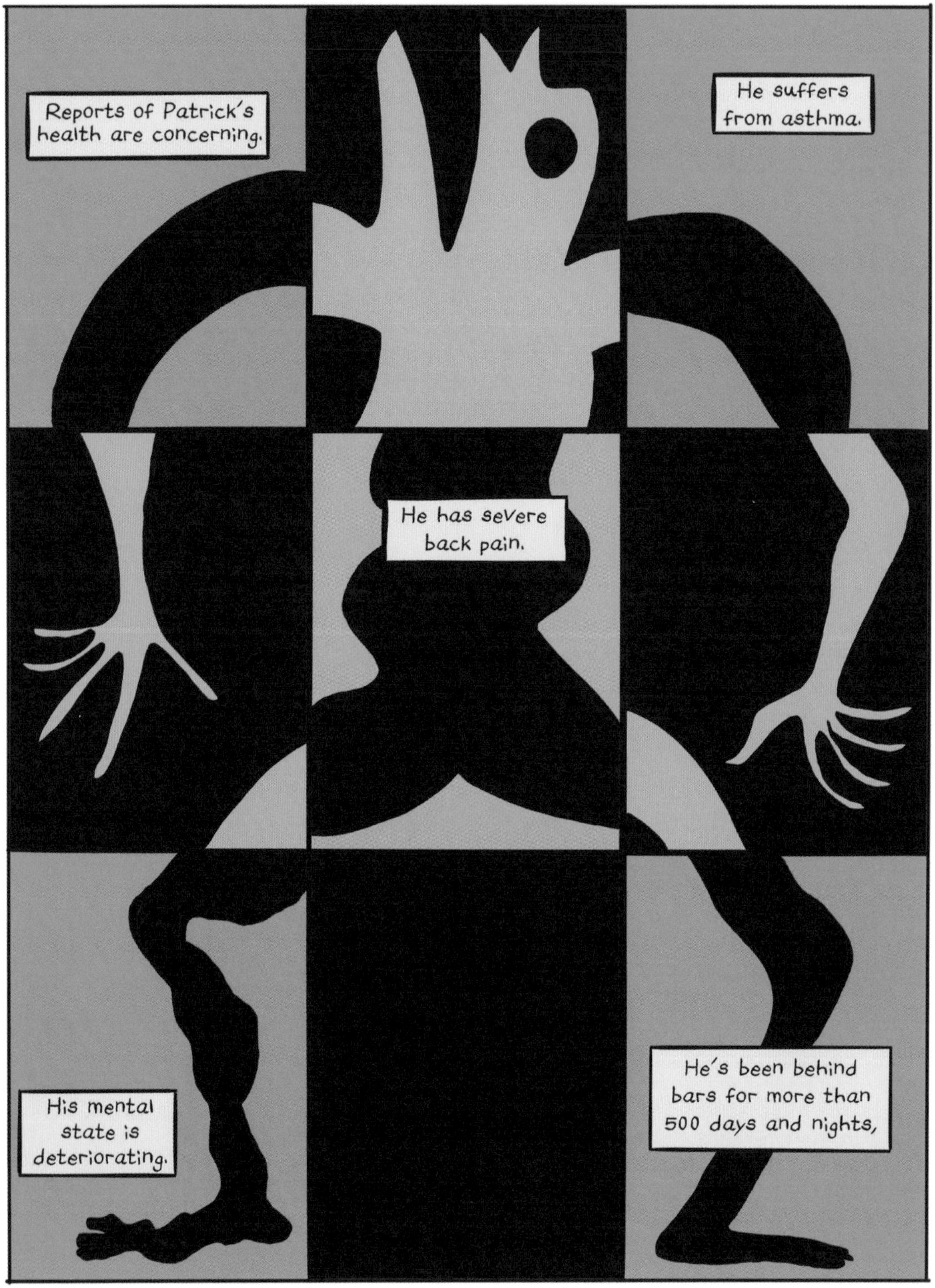
Reports of Patrick's health are concerning.
He suffers from asthma.
He has severe back pain.
His mental state is deteriorating.
He's been behind bars for more than 500 days and nights,

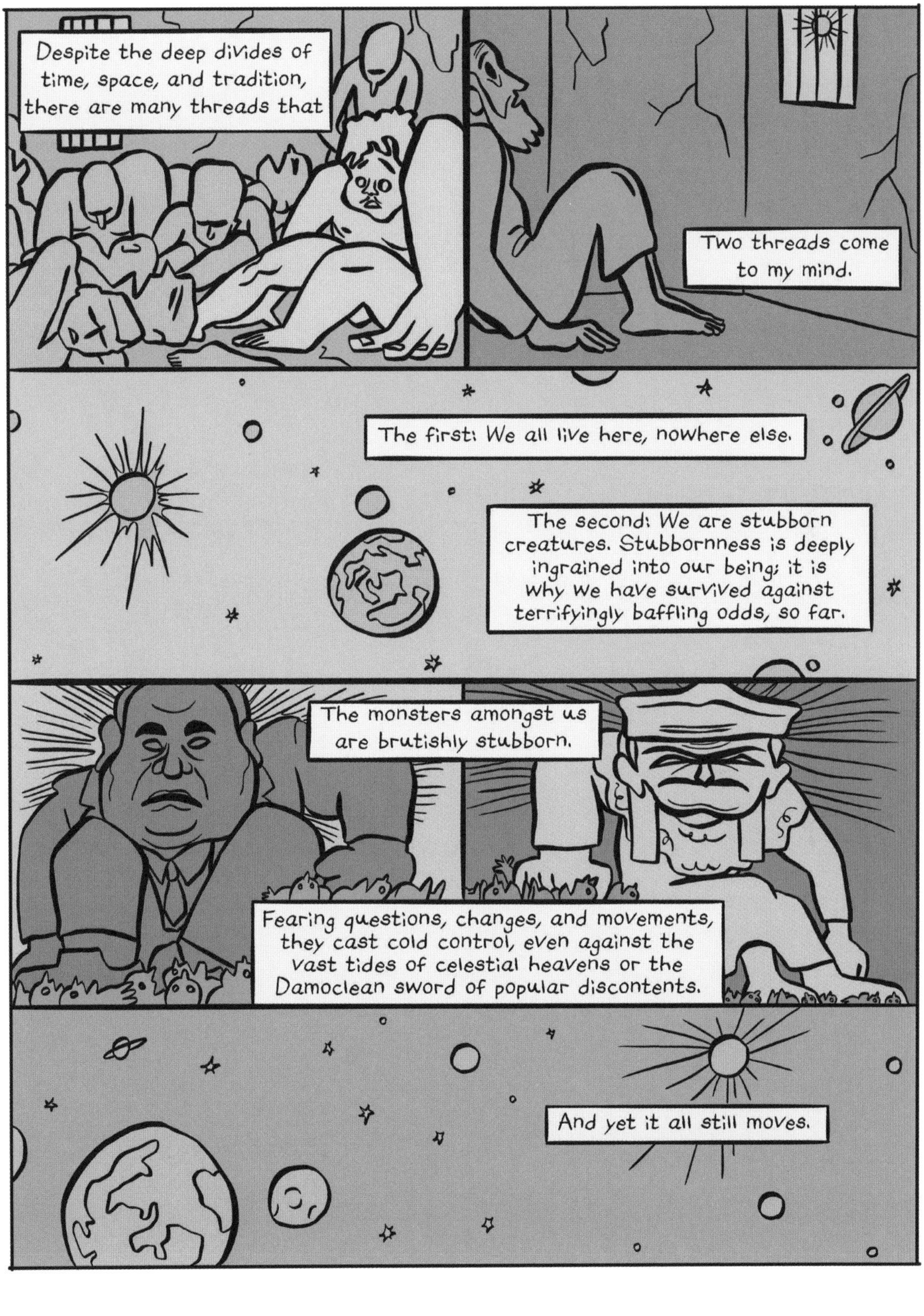
Despite the deep divides of time, space, and tradition, there are many threads that
Two threads come to my mind.
The first: We all live here, nowhere else.
The second: We are stubborn creatures. Stubbornness is deeply ingrained into our being; it is why we have survived against terrifyingly baffling odds, so far.
The monsters amongst us are brutishly stubborn.
Fearing questions, changes, and movements, they cast cold control, even against the vast tides of celestial heavens or the Damoclean sword of popular discontents.
And yet it all still moves.

Patrick Zaki is one among many lives within Egypt's ever-expanding, abusive prison system.

Estimates place the total number of prisoners between 100,000 and 120,000, of whom about 60,000 are political prisoners.

60,000 is a large number to consider, isn't it? Imagine Stadio San Siro in Milan at 75% capacity, filled by silenced voices like Patrick Zaki's.

Without any irony, the Sisi regime denies that a single political prisoner exists in Egypt.

Who are they fooling?

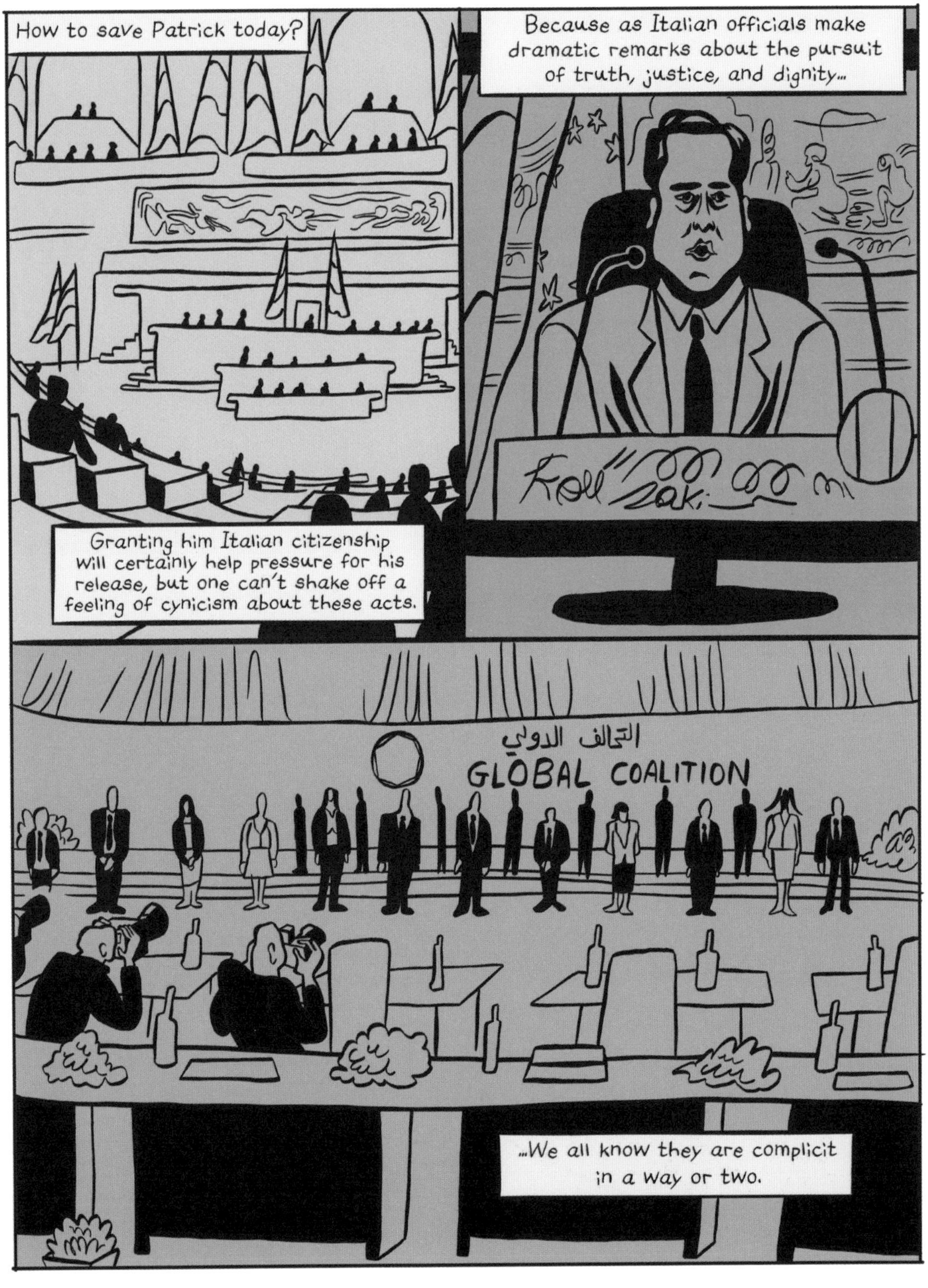
How to save Patrick today?
Granting him Italian citizenship will certainly help pressure for his release, but one can't shake off a feeling of cynicism about these acts.
Because as Italian officials make dramatic remarks about the pursuit of truth, justice, and dignity...
التحالف الدولي
GLOBAL COALITION
...We all know they are complicit in a way or two.

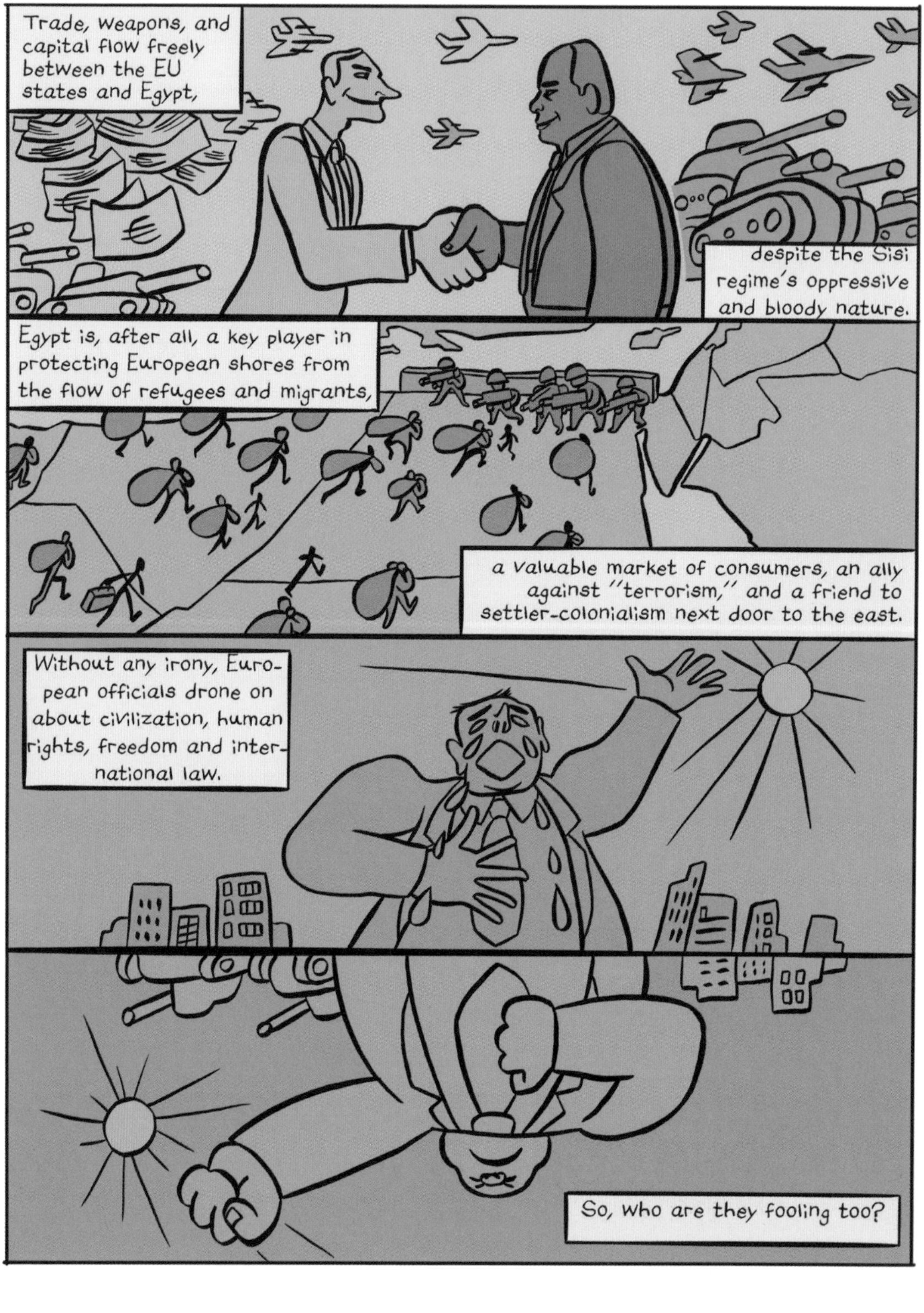

Trade, weapons, and capital flow freely between the EU states and Egypt,
despite the Sisi regime's oppressive and bloody nature.
Egypt is, after all, a key player in protecting European shores from the flow of refugees and migrants,
a valuable market of consumers, an ally against "terrorism," and a friend to settler-colonialism next door to the east.
Without any irony, European officials drone on about civilization, human rights, freedom and international law.
So, who are they fooling too?

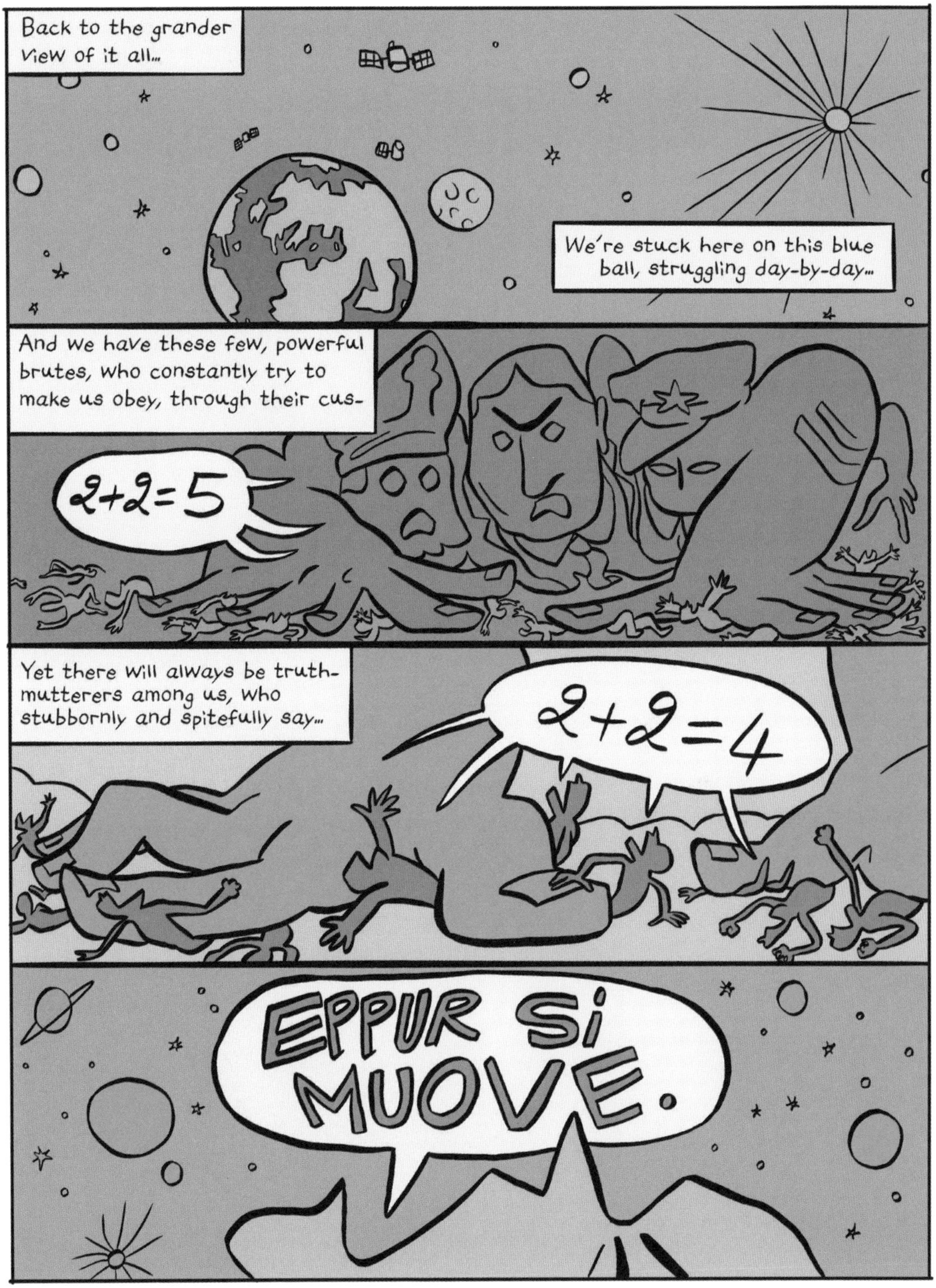
Back to the grander view of it all...
We're stuck here on this blue ball, struggling day-by-day...
And we have these few, powerful brutes, who constantly try to make us obey, through their cus-
2+2=5
Yet there will always be truth-mutterers among us, who stubbornly and spitefully say...
2+2=4
EPPUR SI MUOVE.

6.
SEVENTY YEARS OF CATASTROPHE

Yazan Al-Saadi and Ghadi Ghosn

One of the largest nonviolent Palestinian mobilizations, the Great March of Return (GMR) was launched on March 30, 2018, and lasted until December 27, 2019. These protests demanded the right of return (a right enshrined in international law and various human rights conventions) for Palestinian refugees who were ethnically cleansed from their homes by Zionist forces in 1948 as well as the end of Israel's ongoing illegal blockade of Gaza, which was a form of collective punishment. The GMR also protested the US government's recognition of Jerusalem as the capital of Israel.

The Great March of Return is yet another example of how the Palestinians have stood up to Israel's oppression. It was a massive peaceful action. In response, Israeli forces killed at least 223 Palestinians, including 46 children and medical personnel (including Palestinian nurse Rouzan al-Najjar), and injured more than 36,100, of whom 8,800 were children. Israeli snipers deliberately shot to maim. As a result, many were left unable to walk normally again.

Israel, as usual, permitted these crimes, thus setting the stage for the present-day overt genocide conducted against the Palestinians, after decades of what Israeli historian Ilan Pappé dubbed an "incremental genocide."

This comic was drawn by my trusted partner Ghadi Ghosn.

Page 55: The scene playing out on the TV is of the case of twelve-year-old Muhammad al-Durrah, who was killed on live television on September 30, 2000. The Israelis denied the murder and claimed it was faked (it wasn't). Muhammad's father, Jamal, was also injured and never received justice for the death of his son. Jamal came forward again recently in October 2023 after more of his relatives were killed by Israel in the attack on Gaza. This is one of the many incidents that have been seared into the minds of an entire generation of Palestinians.

Page 56 (top): Ghadi is riffing on an actual photo taken in 1948 of Palestinians being forcibly displaced from their homes. By the end of that war, Zionist forces would successfully depopulate more than four hundred towns and villages across historical Palestine.

Page 56 (bottom): The Israelis like to talk about the miraculous victory they achieved in 1948 over "all Arab armies." Students of history know there was nothing miraculous about it. The Arab armies were fragmented and bankrupt, and they half-heartedly joined the fray after most of the Palestinians were already displaced.

Page 59 (top): Here Ghadi riffs on an actual photo taken in 1967 as Israeli forces prepared to attack and occupy Jerusalem.

Page 60 (top): Another riff on an actual photo taken in March 30, 1976, the launch of the first "Land Day" protests by Palestinians who were able to remain within the 1948 borders that made up Israel. In effect, this community had to deal with an apartheid system and was constantly under attack by the new government formed around them.

Page 60 (bottom): A riff on a photo showing the siege of Beirut in 1982. Israel's siege and attack on Beirut killed nearly thirty thousand people (according to high estimates—some are as low as fifteen thousand) in the course of seven weeks. The attack on Beirut was reportedly what radicalized an individual named Osama bin Laden.

Page 61 (top): Art inspired by another iconic photo, this time from the Second Intifada (uprising). The child throwing the rock at the tank is named Faris Odeh. During the First Intifada, children would often throw stones at tanks, and Israeli soldiers were ordered by Yitzak Rabin, the so-called peacemaker, to "break the bones" of any Palestinian with a rock. Faris Odeh was killed by Israeli forces on November 8, 2000, soon after this photo was taken.

Page 63: The quote from Edward Said is from his essay "Permission to Narrate," which was published in the spring of 1984 in reaction to Israel's attack on Beirut and the West's response to that attack. Not much has changed since then in terms of how Israel operates and how its Western allies respond.

Page 64: A riff on one of the many photos that were taken during the Great March of Return in 2018.

Pages 65–66: The only solution to the Israeli-Palestinian conflict is democratic equality for all. The only way to achieve sustainable peace and justice for every single person in historical Palestine (Jewish, Christian, Muslim, or secular) is to have a shared state with rights protected for all. Anything less will only continue the horrors we are seeing today.

I started paying attention to Palestine while I was in high school in Kuwait. It was September 2000 and the second uprising against the Israeli occupation had kicked off.

Out of all the devastating images on TV at that time — it was the on-camera shooting death of 12-year-old Muhammad al-Durrah on the second day of the uprising which is still frozen in my memory.
More deaths were to come.

A political consciousness was stirred as my young mind was confronted by a blatant example of injustice.
With it came a question:
How does it end?

VOLUME UP

Perhaps it's easier to say how it started.

When the Zionist forces declared the state of Israel on May 14, 1948, they had already expelled Palestinian inhabitants of 220 villages and conquered around 13 percent of historical Palestine.

With bluster and bombast, neighboring Arab countries rushed to defend Palestine. Militarily outmatched, and plagued with infighting, lousy planning, and self-preservation, the Arab forces crumbled before the Zionists.

Alongside the war was a rapid and devastating campaign of ethnic cleansing. By July 1948, 530 towns and main villages and 145 smaller villages were emptied of their inhabitants, 805,000 Palestinians became refugees, and 77 percent of historical Palestine was conquered.

This is known as Al-Nakba, 'The Catastrophe'.

Many more indignities followed. Newly conceived Israeli laws stripped Palestinians of their land, identity, and rights.

Israel adopted a 'free-fire policy' against refugees returning to their homes and fields in areas controlled. 2,700 to 5,000 unarmed Palestinians — dismissively labeled as 'infiltrators' — were killed from 1949-1956.

The Catastrophe rippled across a region already roiling from the fallout of decolonization. A whirlwind followed. Coups. Counter-coups. Counter-counter coups. Cold, hot, boiling wars. Socialism, Ba'athism, Third Worldism, Islamism, and other -isms competed ferociously. Sexual revolutions, oil, and Um Khalthom. Life morphed and lumbered.

Ever-present, the question of Palestine and the Palestinians.

Then came six days in the summer of '67 when Israel launched a surprise attack on Egypt, Syria, and other countries, triggering a second Arab-Israeli war. By its end, Israel had seized more land from Syria, Egypt and Jordan. Hundreds of thousands more joined an exhausted, apparently eternal refugee population.

This is known as Al-Naksa, "The Setback." The uprising that captivated me in high school, a protest against the world's longest military occupation of the lands Israel had seized 33 years earlier, was its bitter fruit.

Frankly, at age 16 I barely knew anything with any certainty. I was aware of Palestine, a people called Palestinians. They were mainly refugees, or were shot on our television screens as we watched.

I clearly had to read more. So I did. One book after another.

Each new book brought new terms and concepts. What seemed complex became simpler to grasp.

And slowly, watching, consuming, and listening,

especially to what the Israeli discourse was saying, I inched forward to an inevitable conclusion.

"The Setback" is a funny phrase. Muted, minimal, like a stumble. But 1967 was a deep plunge. Years of freefall followed. Fighting between the Palestine Liberation Organization and Jordan drove the PLO into a second exile in Lebanon.

There was a fourth Arab-Israeli war. And perhaps a sliver of hope: on March 30, 1976, Palestinians who remained in Israel pushed back, for the first time, and protested against ongoing land expropriations.

A peace deal with Egypt, bought and paid for by the US, promoted Israeli expansionist ambitions. In the civil-war-torn capital of Lebanon, where the PLO was based, Israel saw a chance to strike at the heart of Palestinian resistance and laid siege.

For seven weeks, Israeli forces, aircraft, and navy cut off supplies and shelled Beirut.
Thousands perished and the PLO was again sent into retreat.

In 1987, an Israeli military truck crashed into a car, killing all the Palestinians in it.
What followed was the "Intifada", "The Uprising." There were strikes, boycotts, civil disobedience, and Palestinian children with stones facing a military armed with a nuclear arsenal.

Fearing irrelevance, Palestinian politicians announced a 'peace process' with Israel.

The 'peace process' was more concerned with the process rather than peace. Palestinians under the occupation felt increasingly frustrated and appalled as they watched their inalienable rights, particularly the right to return, being swept away.

A provocation by an Israeli right-winger led to the Second Intifada, which in turn led to further repression by the Israeli military, colonial expansion of Israeli settlements, and a wall — significantly dwarfing the Berlin Wall by height and length — that snakes through and around Palestinian towns, villages, and cities.

Gaza, out of all the Palestinian lands, paid and pays the highest toll. 1.8 million people found themselves trapped in an open-air prison, 141 square miles in size, under a land, air, and sea Israeli-Egyptian blockade.

Gaza suffered three wars since 2008, in which around 3,800 Palestinians were killed (mainly civilians), while 90 Israelis died (mainly military) in total.

The late American-Palestinian academic Edward Said once wrote: "Facts do not at all speak for themselves, but require a socially acceptable narrative to absorb, sustain and circulate them. Such a narrative has to have a beginning and end:

in the Palestinian case, a homeland for the resolution of its exile since 1948."

There are mountains of facts, historical records, and detailed and crosschecked evidence, meticulously gathered together by many hands across time and space, which outline how Zionist forces conducted a pre-planned ethnic cleansing of historical Palestine, which continues to this day.

And at its root, this is a story, like many other stories, encapsulated by one word: Power.

It is no surprise that it was in Gaza where the latest events of 2018 emerged.

Driven by despair at any viable resolution, tens of thousands of Gazans joined the "Great March of Return" and gathered near the border fence. The Israelis were waiting. Like in 1949, they had implemented a 'free-fire policy'.

At the time of this writing, over 90 Palestinians have been killed, and over 9,000 people — men, women, children, the elderly — injured by sniper fire.

The world, like it always does, merely gazes.

So... How can this end?

Let's be frank, we've got the Israelis — a nuclear armed state with an enormously powerful air force— protected and backed politically, militarily, and economically by an international superpower in its ambitions to cement its control of the land and maintain an ethno-national state, discriminatory by its very nature.

On the other side, the Palestinians, fractured, exiled, dispelled, whose core agenda is to struggle for their mere existence and the right to return to their homes lost in 1948 if they choose to.

There is a fundamental moral choice to be made here, and its resolution lies in the hands of the same state - with its backers - that engineered it. This can end with a right to return to lands that were ethnically cleansed, compensation for the harm of innocents, and a process to ensure that everyone within the lands of historical Palestine — regardless of religion, ethnicity, or anything else — has liberty and dignity.

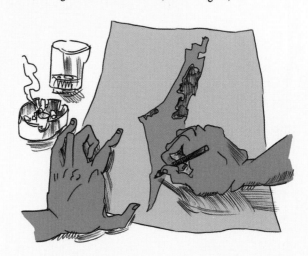

But it is only the Israelis, the ultimate power-holders, who can make that decision to take another path than the one they have taken since 1948.

Until they do, the Palestinian struggle persists, as it has for 70 years. And if that choice is left unmade, I wonder what calamities the next 70 years will bring?

7.
FROM PALESTINE TO TURTLE ISLAND

Yazan Al-Saadi and Sirène Moukheiber

This comic was created with a particular audience in mind: Canadians. It is very hard to have a conversation about Israel in Canada, even within progressive circles, because it's such a fraught topic. There is a growing intolerance of pro-Palestinian demonstrations. And it's difficult to ignore the inherent genocidal and apartheid nature of the Israeli state. I suppose those are the unavoidable characteristics of settler-colonial states, including late-stage ones like the United States, Australia, and, of course, Canada. What differentiates Israel from the rest of its colonial peers is a matter of timing. While, generations ago, the genocidal projects in the United States, Australia, and Canada "successfully" marginalized the Indigenous communities (although the remaining Indigenous communities continue to resist that ongoing annihilation, which should remind us all that the fight never ends), Israel nonetheless remains the last overt settler-colonial state. All of us bear witness to its ongoing genocidal process, streamed live to our phones at this very moment.

Consequently, Israel is at the "cutting edge" of colonialism in practice. It has developed many tools in service to its agenda, such as digital surveillance and hacking, reinterpretations of international law, sophisticated forms of incarceration, and creative ways to kill and maim. Being at the forefront of the practice of genocide ensures that Israel has consistently ranked among the top ten "defense-exporting" countries since the start of the twenty-first century (ranking eighth worldwide, according to the SIPRI Arms Transfers Database, March 2021) and has been expanding in the arms trade and policing market since the 1980s. Remember, this is a nuclear-armed state, smaller than the size of New York, rivaling the arms trade of larger countries like Russia, China, the United States, France, and the United Kingdom.

The police and army in the United States and Canada are well-versed in how to commit brutality and murder, but lately, Israel has refined and elevated the practice, galvanizing other nation-states in turn to learn from them or directly purchase the tools needed to imitate their practices.

The art for this comic is by the sensational Sirène Moukheiber, an artist who excels at dynamic page layouts and playful paneling, with whom I have worked on a number of comics and graphic novels. The narrative is inspired by Maya Angelou's poem "Caged Bird," reprinted here with permission.

Page 70: The Arabic lyrics snaking out of the prison window are from a song often sung by Arab prisoners, and they mean "I enjoy your company. I enjoy your company when you are with me." Many international and local NGOs have been recording the number of Palestinians held by Israel at any given time. There have been thousands.

Page 71: When I was writing this comic, the daring escape of six Palestinian prisoners from Gilboa prison—and their subsequent recapture—was the main story in the news. The quote at the end of this page is allegedly what one of them said to his lawyer after being caught.

Page 72: Forced labor camps were ubiquitous in the 1940s and 1950s. The International Committee of the Red Cross (ICRC) reported on them at the time. The information was at first classified until it was rediscovered and rereleased by Palestinian historian Salman Abu Sitta in 2014.

Page 73: The survivors' quotes are taken from the work of Salman Abu Sitta, author of *Atlas of Palestine*.

Page 74: The statistics mentioned here are collected from a range of sources, including the Institute of Palestine Studies, a 2019 report by the Palestinian Prisoners Committee, and Addameer (www.addameer.org), to name a few.

Page 75: The description of female prisoner abuse is taken from various sources, including reports by the Palestinian Prisoners Committee, Al-Shabaka, and Human Rights Watch.

Page 77: A growing body of research shows how central Israel has become to the global arms, surveillance, and policing industries. The majority of Israel's production in this industry (about 75 percent) is made not for internal use but for export.

Page 78: The link between Ejaz Choudry's murder and the fact that the Canadian police had trained with Israel has been revealed by the likes of the Canadian BDS Coalition, while the other connections noted here between Canada and Israel were from a 2015 brief by Independent Jewish Voices (https://ijvcanada .org/wp-content/uploads/2015/03/Challenging-Israeli-Canadian-Global-Pacifi cation-no-Links.pdf) during an anti-militarization campaign.

Page 79: The information on this page is also taken from the Independent Jewish Voices 2015 brief, which nicely summarizes the different ties between Canada and Israel. There are mountains of these pamphlets, briefs, reports, and info-graphics that show the depth of Israel's incremental genocide and its place in the larger international order.

FROM PALESTINE TO TURTLE ISLAND:
THE CAGED BIRD SINGS OF FREEDOM

Written by: Yazan Al-Saadi | Art by: Sirène Moukheiber

THE FREE BIRD THINKS OF ANOTHER BREEZE

AND THE TRADE WINDS SOFT THROUGH THE SIGHING TREES

AND THE FAT WORMS WAITING ON A DAWN BRIGHT LAWN

AND HE NAMES THE SKY HIS OWN

BUT A CAGED BIRD STANDS ON THE GRAVE OF DREAMS

HIS SHADOW SHOUTS ON A NIGHTMARE SCREAM

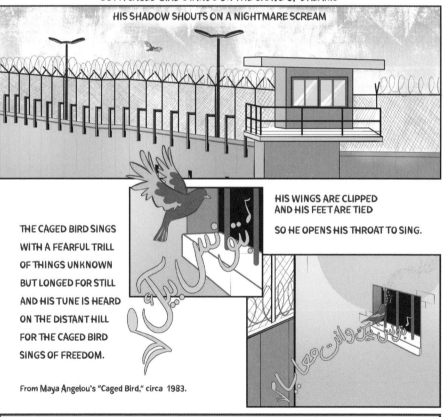

HIS WINGS ARE CLIPPED
AND HIS FEET ARE TIED

SO HE OPENS HIS THROAT TO SING.

THE CAGED BIRD SINGS
WITH A FEARFUL TRILL
OF THINGS UNKNOWN
BUT LONGED FOR STILL
AND HIS TUNE IS HEARD
ON THE DISTANT HILL
FOR THE CAGED BIRD
SINGS OF FREEDOM.

From Maya Angelou's "Caged Bird," circa 1983.

Around 4,650 Palestinians, 200 of whom are children,
are held by Israel in its modern-day dungeons.

The plight of Palestinian prisoners came into focus after the daring escape of six prisoners from a high-tech maximum security compound - **Gilboa prison** - located in northern historical Palestine.

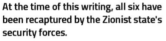
BREAKING NEWS

It took a rusty spoon, coupled with patience, planning, effort, and a spiteful stubborn desire for liberty, to undermine
– for a sliver of a moment –
the frail illusion of Israeli omnipotence and supremacy over Palestinian lives.

At the time of this writing, all six have been recaptured by the Zionist state's security forces.

Israel's revenge for this Palestinian defiance was brutal and swift.
Not only were the prisoners' family members and almost a hundred Palestinians arrested as a form of collective punishment and pressure, the recaptured men were also tortured – bones broken, faces cut and bruised, and their sleep-deprived, naked bodies forced into inhumane stress positions.

Despite being recaptured and experiencing further abuses, according to one of their lawyers, these six men expressed their joy that they were able to be outside the prison walls under the open blue sky.

FOR THE FIRST TIME SINCE I WAS TAKEN PRISONER 22 YEARS AGO, I WAS ABLE TO EAT PRICKLY PEARS FROM A FIELD. IT WAS THE FIRST TIME IN MY LIFE I WAS ABLE TO WALK AROUND AND SEE HISTORIC PALESTINE.

Mahmoud Al-Arda

Since the launch of its incremental genocide against Palestinians in 1947-48,

Israel has been, and continues to be, a carceral state par excellence.

Between
1948 and 1955

Zionist forces had established at least

22 CONCENTRATION & LABOR CAMPS

4 OF WHICH WERE "OFFICIAL".

One Palestinian survivor, **Moussa** (or Moses in English), described decades later what he witnessed at that time.

THEY TOOK US FROM ALL THE VILLAGES THAT WERE AROUND US: AL-BI'NA, DEIR AL-ASAD, NAHAF, AL-RAMA, AND EILABUN. THEY TOOK 4 YOUNG MEN AND SHOT THEM DEAD...THEY DROVE US ON FOOT. IT WAS HOT. WE WERE NOT ALLOWED TO DRINK.

Another survivor, **Kamal Ghattas**, noted an interesting ideological irony that occurred in one of the concentration camps.

WE HAD A FIGHT WITH OUR JAILERS. FOUR HUNDRED OF US CONFRONTED 100 SOLDIERS. THEY BROUGHT REINFORCEMENTS. THREE OF MY FRIENDS AND I WERE TAKEN TO A CELL. THEY THREATENED TO SHOOT US. ALL NIGHT WE SANG THE COMMUNIST ANTHEM. THEY TOOK THE FOUR OF US TO UMM KHALED CAMP. THE ISRAELIS WERE AFRAID OF THEIR IMAGE IN EUROPE. OUR CONTACT WITH OUR CENTRAL COMMITTEE AND MAPAM [SOCIALIST ISRAELI PARTY] SAVED US ...

I MET A RUSSIAN OFFICER AND TOLD HIM THEY TOOK US FROM OUR HOMES ALTHOUGH WE WERE NON-COMBATANTS WHICH WAS AGAINST THE GENEVA CONVENTIONS. WHEN HE KNEW I WAS A COMMUNIST, HE EMBRACED ME AND SAID:

COMRADE, I HAVE TWO BROTHERS IN THE RED ARMY. LONG LIVE STALIN. LONG LIVE MOTHER RUSSIA.

The biggest irony, which continues to this day, is that many of the Zionist prison guards were themselves prisoners in Nazi Germany's concentration and labor camps a few years prior.

Israel's carceral system expanded considerably after it launched the 1967 war to conquer more land.

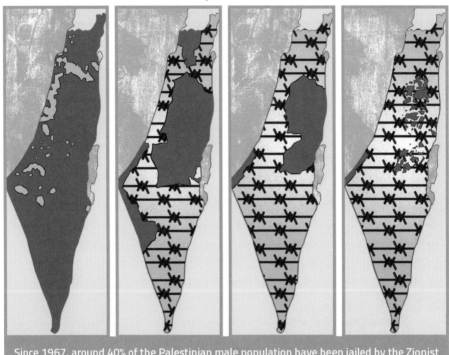

Since 1967, around 40% of the Palestinian male population have been jailed by the Zionist state. In total, at least one million Palestinians have been arrested since 1967, including

17 000
WOMEN

50 000
CHILDREN

& MORE THAN
54 000

PALESTINIANS UNDERWENT
ADMINISTRATIVE DETENTION

This is the highest rate of incarceration in the world, with around 15-20 Palestinians on average arrested by Israeli forces every day.

At least 226 detainees have died inside Israeli prisons, all of whom reportedly experienced "some form of physical or psychological torture, moral abuse, and cruel treatment" before they perished.

Palestinian women, in particular, are brutally targeted by Israel. They are threatened with rape and sexual abuse by the guards and their interrogators; their cultural and societal practices are actively disrespected; they have experienced physical and psychological torture during the detention process and are often deprived of any family visitations.

Their overall and specific medical needs are disregarded – hence, around 25% of Palestinian female prisoners suffer from treatable diseases.

Detained pregnant Palestinian women are forced to give birth, shackled in metal chains, with no family allowed. After giving birth, they are immediately transferred – **with the baby** – back to their overcrowded, unhygienic prison cells.

IS IT ANY WONDER, THEN, THAT PALESTINIAN WOMEN ARE THE MELODY OF RESISTANCE?
They were the ones to launch, back in 1970, one of the first hunger strikes of the Palestinian prisoners' movement. Ever since, they have consistently joined or led hunger strikes and protest actions throughout all the Israeli prisons, and are the bearers of revolutionary education.

As **Khalida Jarrar,** a Palestinian feminist, leftist, Parliamentarian, and recently released prisoner, who had experienced frequent administrative detention since 2014 by Israel, once said:

IN PRISON, WE CHALLENGE THE ABUSIVE PRISON GUARD TOGETHER, WITH THE SAME WILL AND DETERMINATION TO BREAK HIM SO THAT HE DOES NOT BREAK US...

PRISON IS THE ART OF EXPLORING POSSIBILITIES; IT IS A SCHOOL THAT TRAINS YOU TO SOLVE DAILY CHALLENGES USING THE SIMPLEST AND MOST CREATIVE MEANS, WHETHER IT BE FOOD PREPARATION, MENDING OLD CLOTHES OR FINDING COMMON GROUND SO THAT WE MAY ALL ENDURE AND SURVIVE TOGETHER.

FOR PALESTINIANS, THE PRISON IS A MICROCOSM OF THE MUCH LARGER STRUGGLE OF A PEOPLE WHO REFUSE TO BE ENSLAVED ON THEIR OWN LAND, AND WHO ARE DETERMINED TO REGAIN THEIR FREEDOM, WITH THE SAME WILL AND VIGOR CARRIED BY ALL TRIUMPHANT, ONCE-COLONIZED NATIONS.

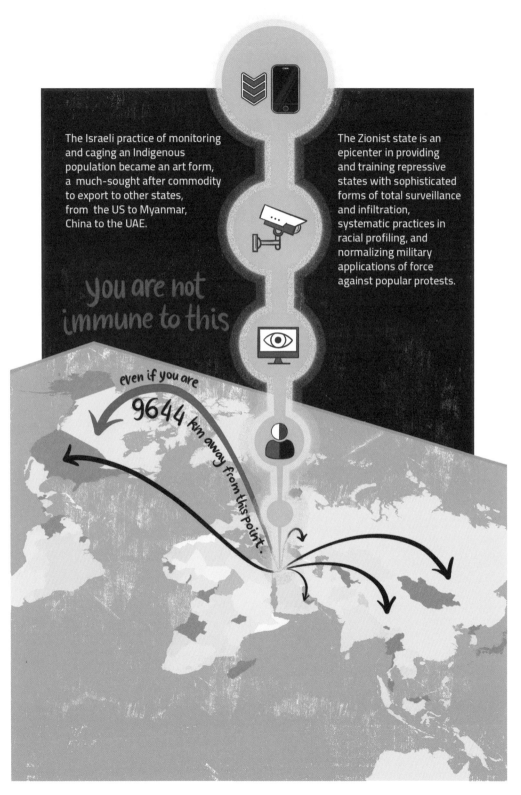

The Israeli practice of monitoring and caging an Indigenous population became an art form, a much-sought after commodity to export to other states, from the US to Myanmar, China to the UAE.

The Zionist state is an epicenter in providing and training repressive states with sophisticated forms of total surveillance and infiltration, systematic practices in racial profiling, and normalizing military applications of force against popular protests.

you are not immune to this

even if you are 9644 km away from this point.

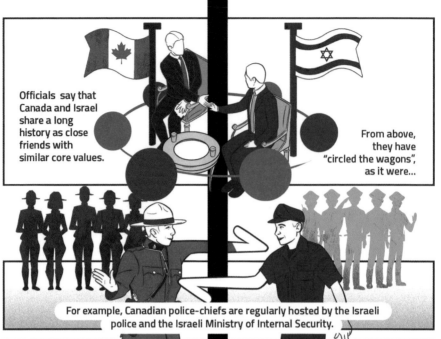

Officials say that Canada and Israel share a long history as close friends with similar core values.

From above, they have "circled the wagons", as it were...

For example, Canadian police-chiefs are regularly hosted by the Israeli police and the Israeli Ministry of Internal Security.

As these forces learn from each other, the result is bloody for the rest of us. Think of **the case of Ejaz Choudry**, who suffered from schizophrenia and was killed in his own home by the Peel Regional Police on June 20, 2020.

The blatant misuse of power and excessive use of deadly force is enshrined in the training programs between the Israeli and Canadian security forces.

You, me, any of us could be Choudry...

Black and Indigenous peoples in
Canadian Population   Federal Prisons

50%
25%

Similarly, Senstar – **owned by Israel's Magal Security Systems** – has a major manufacturing facility in Carp, Ontario. It is a key provider of perimeter security equipment for the Canadian Correctional Service.

The Canadian Correctional Service is notoriously discriminatory – in which Indigenous and Black people account for only **4.8%** and **3.5%** of the Canadian population yet make up **25.5%** and **8.7%** respectively in federal prisons.

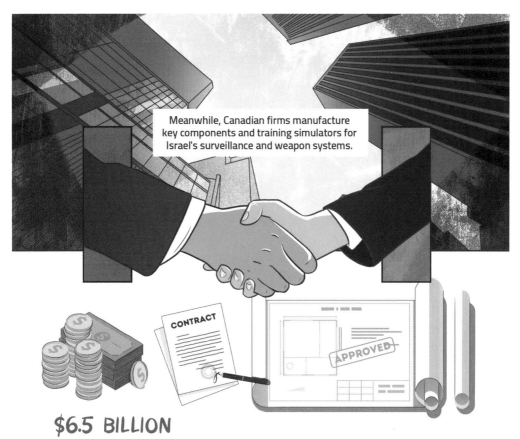

Meanwhile, Canadian firms manufacture key components and training simulators for Israel's surveillance and weapon systems.

$6.5 BILLION

are invested by Canadian contracts with Israel - including the Canadian Pension Plan, Ontario Teachers Pension Plan, Quebec Pension Plan, the Public Sector Pension Investments, and the Ontario Municipal Employees.

Oh yes, Canada has been complicit since the very beginning of Israel's incremental genocide of the Palestinians, and still is today....

**DO YOU SEE HOW WE ARE ALL BONDED TOGETHER
– TURTLE ISLAND TO PALESTINE –
BY MISERABLE HOOK OR SPITEFUL CROOK?**

DO YOU SEE THE LARGER CAGE ENCASING US?

DO YOU SEE THE CHAINS FORGED AROUND OUR NECKS?

THE POWERS-THAT-BE ARE PLANNING WICKED DESIGNS
FOR THIS NEW CENTURY;
SHOULDN'T WE WORK TOGETHER TO RESPOND
BEFORE IT'S TOO LATE?

DO YOU NOT HEAR THE SONG BEING SUNG?

LISTEN, DON'T YOU HEAR IT?

WITH ITS URGENT PITCH,
ROLLING RHYTHM,
AND POWERFUL TUNE

AN EARWORM, WITH A CRISP, CLEAR VOW:
WALLS SHALL SHAKE, BARS WILL BOW.

8.
CAIRO UNDER THE CRACKDOWN

Yazan Al-Saadi and Ganzeer

Since Egyptian army chief General Abdel Fattah Sisi's 2013 coup against the Muslim Brotherhood, things have regressed in Egypt. Never in its history has there been such large-scale oppression. Today, Egypt is the third-leading jailer of journalists and prisoners of conscience worldwide. When I was in Egypt in 2018 for more than a month, it was clear that the country was still haunted by a number of troubling incidents from previous years.

First, there was the Raba'a Square massacre on August 14, 2013, in which over one thousand people were killed in the span of a few hours. It was, as described by Human Rights Watch, "one of the world's largest killings of demonstrators in a single day in recent history."

Second was the hidden war in the Sinai Peninsula by the Egyptian army against tribes, militias, and other armed groups. To date, the events of that war are obscured, but there are multiple credible reports of extrajudicial killings by the Egyptian state, the destruction of people's homes, and other abuses. In Cairo, people could only talk about these events in whispers.

Third, in 2017, Mashrou' Leila, a famous and popular Lebanese band, held a concert in Cairo at which the rainbow flag was flown by an Egyptian socialist and queer activist named Sarah Hegazi. This unleashed a massive political and social crackdown on the queer community, including Sarah, with complete silence from all of the progressive and leftist groups on the ground.

This comic captures the dark feelings of paranoia and dissent I experienced during my time in Egypt. The artist here is the renowned Egyptian artist Ganzeer, whose political street art gained an immense following during the 2011 Egyptian uprising. Ganzeer was later forced to leave the country. In solidarity with the queer community, we used the colors of the rainbow flag in this comic.

Page 85 (middle right): I mentioned Giulio Regeni previously in this collection. His death was on the minds of many researchers and academics in Egypt at the time.

Page 85 (bottom): This actually happened while I was meeting my friend, and I could not ignore the paranoia that everyone understandably felt at the time. It reminded me of Syria in the 1980s.

Page 86: An Egyptian friend and leftist activist once took me on a tour of Cairo and described the events he had experienced, including the massacre in Raba'a. It was an opportunity to reflect on the failures of the uprising and the toll it has taken on people like himself.

Pages 87–88 (top left): The juxtaposition of these two gatherings reflects an interesting class (or privilege) dynamic at work. It seemed to me that those with less privilege had more hope about the potential for change.

Pages 88–89: I chose this ending because it offers a lesson on the tenuous nature of state control, even in a space like security-heavy Egypt. Those in power are not always immune to public opinion. Things can turn against them very, very quickly.

Cairo, the English name for Al-Qahira, literally means "vanquisher." It's also translated as "victorious" or "man-breaker."

The word has an old origin: Khere-Ohe or "Place of Combat," a reference to the battle between the ancient Egyptian gods Horus and Seth.

It is the largest city across the African continent and West Asian region combined.

Cairo has more than 20 million residents.

Nearly eight years after the fall of Mubarak, and four years into the iron rule of President Sisi, the city has an air of palpable paranoia, despair, and defiance.

Things are festering in the state of Egypt.

The state has used widespread arrests, crackdowns, and torture to target liberals, leftists, feminists, academics, journalists, Islamists, and more.

Within this context, I met an old friend who was researching Female Genital Mutilation in Egypt and the state's failure in addressing it.

BASED ON *AVAILABLE NUMBERS,* IT'S AROUND *90% OF ALL EGYPTIAN WOMEN* THAT HAD TO GO THROUGH SOME FORM OF *F.G.M.*

!

YEAH, IT'S *ENTRENCHED HISTORICALLY* AS A SOCIAL AND *CULTURAL* PRACTICE, PUSHED BY SOCIETY, A GOVERNMENT THAT NEVER *SERIOUSLY* TACKLES THE ISSUE, AND OTHER THINGS - IT'S *SUPER* HIGH.

EASY TO WORK ON?

YES.

HORRIBLE.

DEPENDS.

YOU HEAR ABOUT WHAT *HAPPENED* TO *THE ITALIAN?*

Giulio Regeni.

Italian PhD student who conducted research on unions in Egyptian workplaces.

Tortured to death in 2016.

Suspected killer: government security forces.

EXACTLY, AND...YAZAN... EVEN *NOW,* I'M...

I *DON'T FEEL* COMFORTABLE.

WHAT DO YOU MEAN?

7 O'CLOCK.

HUH?

IT'S 1 PM.

I'M CONFUSED.

7 O'CLOCK! LOOK.

LOOK!

I DON'T THINK HE'S WHAT YOU THINK HE IS.

HOW DO YOU *KNOW*?

BECAUSE... WE AREN'T *ARRESTED* YET?

Am I right?

One evening, a friend takes me on a tour of the "hot spots of the 2011 Revolution." We meet after work at Tahrir square.

And we walk, his memories guiding our steps.

THERE! AH, I REMEMBER THE SMELL OF *TEAR GAS* IN THE AIR.

AND *THERE!* THAT'S WHERE A RELATIVE LIVED IN AN APARTMENT *OVERLOOKING* THE SQUARE. HE *IMMEDIATELY* OPENED HIS BALCONY UP FOR PEOPLE TO *FILM* AND TAKE PHOTOS.

ALSO *THERE!* I REMEMBER WHEN PEOPLE WERE SHARING WIFI, GIVING FOOD, HELPING OUT.

LOOK, *THERE!* HAHA! WE *SURROUNDED* THAT *GOVERNMENT BUILDING.* THEY LOOKED SCARED.

AH, *THERE!* THE BATON *CRACKED* MY HEAD. THINGS WENT BLACK. AND THERE WAS *BLOOD.*

For a brief moment, I see smoky figments of what he's describing.

As soon as I set foot into Cairo, I was whisked away to dinner.

THERE'S *TENSION* IN THE AIR. BUT NOT MUCH TO DO ABOUT IT.

EVERYONE'S TOO *SCARED* AND *EXHAUSTED* WITH LIFE.

TRAUMA AFTER *RABA'A?*

AND THEN SOME.

Raba'a massacre. August 14, 2013. "One of the world's largest killings of demonstrators in a single day in recent history" according to HRW.

Official count of the dead: 600.

Unofficial count: More than 2,500.

PRICES GOING UP.

LIFE'S *HARDER.*

CAN'T TALK MUCH ABOUT THE *WAR* IN *NORTHERN SINAI* TOO.

Insurgency in Sinai. Between the military's "Scorched Earth" policy and the militants' indiscriminate attacks, the civilian dead range from 2,300 to 4,800.

At a friend's place later.

A gathering of assorted young writers, diplomats, photographers, and NGO workers.

Obviously we'd end up talking politics.

THERE WAS *SO MUCH HOPE* DURING THE REVOLUTION.

2011 WAS A *LONG* TIME AGO.

IT'S *ALL* GONE NOW.

IT'S A *DISASTER EVERYWHERE* IN THE *REGION.*

BUT..?

NO BUTS.

PRACTICALLY SPEAKING, PEOPLE ARE *EXHAUSTED*, AND YOU CAN'T FORGET THE LEVEL OF *CONTROL*.

There are tens of thousands of political prisoners, many sentenced through military courts. Freedom of assembly and expression has been curtailed, while extrajudicial killings and forcible disappearances have increased.

Next day, at the office.

HEHE.

My colleague shows me a Facebook post from the Egyptian Ministry of Defense.

GO ON, READ THE *COMMENTS*.

URGENT | The Ministry of Defense calls on all Egyptians on social media to do their patriotic duty and send in the names of traitors critisizing our beautiful nation.

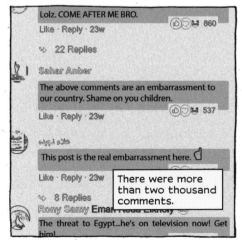

Lolz. COME AFTER ME BRO.
Like · Reply · 23w   860
    22 Replies

Sahar Anber
The above comments are an embarrassment to our country. Shame on you children.
Like · Reply · 23w   537

This post is the real embarrassment here.
Like · Reply · 23w
    8 Replies

There were more than two thousand comments.

Rony Samy Emad

The threat to Egypt...he's on television now! Get him!

HAH HAHAHA!

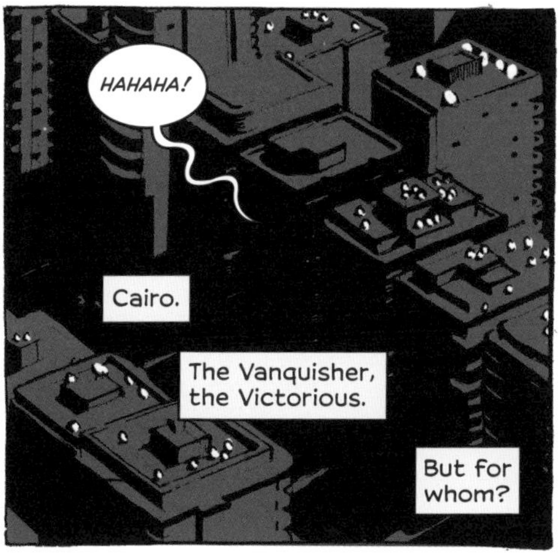
HAHAHA!
Cairo.
The Vanquisher, the Victorious.
But for whom?

9.
AN UPRISING IN SUDAN

Yazan Al-Saadi and Enas Satir

At the end of 2018 and in early 2019, an uprising broke out in Sudan against Omar al-Bashir, who had been in power since 1993 and ruled over several genocides in that country, especially in Darfur. In Sudan, the lines of Arab and African are blurred. It is a country with a long history of political activism and constant civil dissent in the face of oppression. During the uprising in 2018–19, the Sudanese armed forces (likely inspired by their Egyptian counterparts) deposed al-Bashir, placed him under house arrest, and ultimately sentenced him. He remains in detention to this day, along with other figures from the regime.

Today, Sudan is being ripped apart in a civil war between the ruling military junta, headed by General Abdul Fattah al-Burhan, and a rival military faction called the Rapid Support Forces (RSF), composed of Janjaweed militias and headed by Mohamed Hamdan Dagalo (Hemedti). Each party in this conflict is backed by various regional and international powers, and each has committed significant crimes against humanity, including killings, torture, rape, disappearances, and theft. More than twelve thousand people have been killed in Sudan since war erupted between the RSF and the Sudanese army on April 15, 2023.

This comic was drawn by the brilliant Sudanese illustrator Enas Satir, who is currently based in Canada and with whom I was very proud to collaborate.

Page 92 (bottom): Enas is riffing on one of the many photos that came out of the Sudanese uprising at the time. This photo was from Atbara.

Page 94 (top): It is important to note that many of the regimes in the region often quickly align with each other regardless of ideological or other disputes. For all of them, it would seem, the biggest enemy is the people.

Page 94 (middle): Enas's brilliant rendition of "hear no evil, speak no evil, and see no evil."

Page 94 (bottom): Despite there being a warrant for his arrest in 2009 for crimes against humanity, Omar al-Bashir was rehabilitated by the Obama administration not long after that.

Page 95 (middle): I had met Asil during my time with Doctors Without Borders and wanted to honor her, her family, and her community by giving her a space to articulate her thoughts.

Page 96 (top): In the 1960s and 1980s, at the height of Sudan's military dictatorship, the Sudanese people managed to launch two major uprisings that resulted in some change.

Pages 96 (bottom)–98: To this day, the Sudanese people still find a way to resist the violent regime.

In December 2018, Sudanese dictator Omar al-Bashir became the first Arab leader to visit Bashar al-Assad in Syria since the outbreak of that country's civil war.

With great irony, al-Bashir's return to Sudan was welcomed with a resurgent uprising of its own, calling for the end of his 30-year rule.

Al-Bashir's totalitarian regime has presided over horrendous civil wars in Darfur and South Sudan and the secession of about a third of the country.

He has reportedly also stolen $9 billion of the nation's wealth while initiating disastrous neo-liberal economic and austerity policies.

While sporadic protests had been happening in Sudan for some time, a turning point came in Atbara, a city of more than 100,000 residents five hours north-east from the Sudanese capital, Khartoum.

Protests on December 19 over rising bread and fuel prices quickly escalated into calls for the Bashir regime to fall and spread to other villages, towns, and cities, including Khartoum.

Unsurprisingly,
Omar al-Bashir is defiant.

The aging dictator relies on the same old talking points— a foreign conspiracy is afoot, that it's either 'stability' with him or a 'chaos' if he leaves.

Meanwhile, the regime's repressive apparatus is in overdrive.

Violence is employed to disperse peaceful gatherings and the internet has been cut. Authorities search homes and hospitals for dissenters, killing some people in their hunt.

OMDURMAN HOSPITAL

At the time of this writing, at least 50 people have been killed, including children.

WOMEN'S PRISON

Jails burst at the seams. Thousands have been arrested, ranging from academics, activists, and journalists to opposition figures, feminists, union leaders, and laypeople.

Despite a pending International Criminal Court (ICC) arrest warrant for five counts of crimes against humanity and two counts of war crimes during the war in Darfur, al-Bashir has a wide range of regional and international backers.

Rulers in countries like Saudi and Qatar, Turkey and Syria, Egypt and Ethiopia have quickly aligned in expressing support for him.

Powerful nations like the EU, US, China, and Russia are silent or mumble half-hearted concerns about the situation in Sudan.

Yet their financial, political, and military backing of al-Bashir endures.

Al-Bashir's international 'rehabilitation' occurred in 2015 thanks to Barack Obama, in one of his last acts as US president. It was reward for al-Bashir's support of US counter-terrorism efforts, notably hosting a massive CIA office in Khartoum.

Meanwhile, the ICC warrant lingers unanswered.

Sudan also plays a key role as a barrier to asylum seekers and refugees heading to Europe. Italian officials, for example, are funding the Janjaweed –a government– backed militia involved in Darfur's genocide – to act as border guards between Sudan and eastern Africa.

Sudan's resources also present massive commercial investment opportunities that trump other concerns. It is the world's largest exporter of gum arabic – a crucial binding agent for everyday household goods from food and medicine to industry and art.

This is Asil Sidahmed, a good friend currently living in Belgium.

Before we talk I ask her if she's afraid about sharing her name.

I'm not because my family was exiled since the 1980s, with many others. It would be disrespectful for my family and friends risking their lives protesting inside Sudan today.

I love her for this bravery.

-ME: What makes this protest movement different?

-ASIL: It's ordinary people. It's broad-based. It's not elitist. It hasn't been led by any professional association, the Twitterati, the bourgeois groups, or the political parties – and there are more than 90 political parties in Sudan.

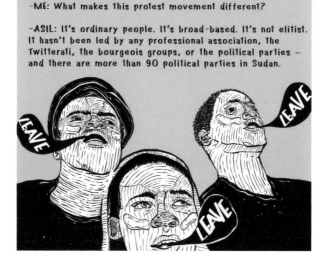

The Sudanese have a rich and long history of actively overthrowing their rulers.

They did so in the 1960s and 1980s when military dictatorships in the West Asian and North African region were at their zenith, and opposition seemed like an impossible dream.

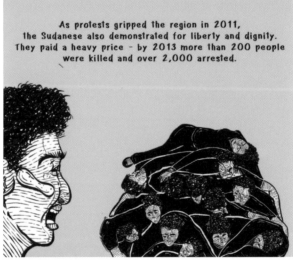

As protests gripped the region in 2011, the Sudanese also demonstrated for liberty and dignity. They paid a heavy price – by 2013 more than 200 people were killed and over 2,000 arrested.

Despite the al-Bashir regime's brutality, cracks in his grip on power have been appearing.

And today, the old dictator faces the largest protests since his 1989 coup.

What are the challenges for the protest movement?

Sudanese face many challenges. We need to identify what makes us Sudanese, who are our allies, where does a pluralist society fit in? We have a lot of unlearning to do. We have to unlearn all the distinctions that fermented disunity and caused us to fight each other. We can't imagine a better inclusive future without first removing this regime.

What's ironic...the so-called president and his regime are so arrogant, so greedy, so heavy-handed, that they, most of all, are creating their own downfall.

Asil and I end our conversation with a toast. She with her wine, me with my whisky.

We toast the uprising in Sudan and a better future for us all.

Will the protests succeed? And who will take power if Bashir falls? Despite the will of foreign powers and their own dictator, the story of Sudan will be dictated by the hands of the Sudanese. They decided what their past was, they are deciding what their present is, and they will decide what their future will be.

10.
THE DICTATOR OR THE EMPEROR

Yazan Al-Saadi and Ghadi Ghosn

This comic grapples with the question of national sovereignty and whether it's better to be ruled by a domestic dictator or an external empire. The two nations I'm considering here are Cuba and Syria. I wanted to reflect these thoughts via my own personal experiences over the years. The first goes back to my time as an exchange student in Havana. Young Cubans were adamant that while it would be a bad idea to succumb to US imperialism, the country wasn't much better off in the long run with Fidel Castro and his regime. This was the first time my preconceived notions were challenged, and I have always remembered how I responded that day. It finally came to a head years later, when I found myself on the opposite side of the table when discussing Syria with a major Lebanese intellectual.

Ultimately, I had to evolve my thinking. The idea of choosing the "lesser evil" between a domestic dictator or an external empire is a logical fallacy. Rather, the choice between a dictator and an emperor is only a non-choice that will lead to tragic ends in multiple ways.

The artist here is Ghadi Ghosn, whose use of symmetry in panel designs and color schemes worked very well with the themes of this comic.

Page 101 (top left): The genocide in Darfur trended in the Western media for a short time (before disappearing altogether), and savage torture methods used by US soldiers on Iraqis in Abu Ghraib also came to light. In both of these cases, none of those who ordered these crimes has been held accountable.

Page 102: The notion of "being realistic" when talking politics is absolute nonsense. It has less to do with finding comprehensive solutions than it does with acquiescing to processes that are convenient for those in power.

Page 103 (bottom left): The bar here was a famous place in East Beirut known as Coop D'État in the Mar Mikhael district. Years later, the bar would close down after the Beirut port explosion in 2020.

Late spring of 2004. The horrors of Abu Gharib were coming to light. GMAIL and Facebook had just appeared. Darfour was news, but would soon be forgotten.

Then, I found myself on a university exchange course, whisked away from a small Canadian city, Kingston, to the grand city of **Havana**, Cuba.

We were around 20 students sent for around three weeks to learn about Cuban society and its history, politics, economic system, philosophy, and culture. I hesitated about going.

It was my parents that convinced me. Both engineers who left Syria in the late 1970s for better economic opportunities, travel was an important privilege. They never hesitated in taking or encouraging their children to see new places.

I spent most of the time hanging out with a bunch of Cuban university students.

We bonded over politics. A micro-manifestation of the nonaligned movement; me representing the Arab contingent, and they, the Latino side. We had common beef with the U.S. and its brutal foreign policy.

One conversation with a student around my age has stuck in my mind.

You guys have it good after the 1959 revolution. Fuck that corrupt lackey Batista and the exploitation of his regime, selling your resources and blood to corporations.
Castro liberated the country. It's amazing.
That's true ,,, But Castro is now old.
Old! So what? Castro brought in free health care, free education, encouraged culture!
That's all great. There has to be more. Don't forget there is still a cost. There is still control, surveillance...
We can't talk as openly. We're not as free as we should be.
Well yeah! There's a threat 90 miles from your island. How many times have the U.S. tried to overthrow the country and bring it back under its control? How many crazy bombings,
assassination attempts, the blockade ?!
I'm aware of all that. We have to fight against these threats. That doesn't mean we're denied our dreams, right? We can do both.
YOU GOTTA BE REALISTIC!
Be realistic!
THE STRUGGLE AGAINST IMPERIALISM ISN'T GOING TO BE PERFECT. SACRIFICES HAVE TO BE MADE! IT'S NOT THE TIME FOR CHANGE.
But-
there was a moment of awkward silence...

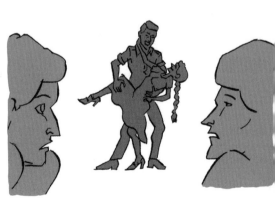

Late spring of 2014. The hopes of the Arab uprisings were fading, muted by a massive counter-revolution supported by the powers-that-be. ISIS burst onto the scene; the US's War on Terror wasn't going well. Facebook had bought WhatsApp. Ebola was news, soon to be forgotten.

Then, I found myself moving from Kuwait to Beirut, to work as a journalist with an English section of a quasi-leftist Lebanese newspaper.

I wanted a change from the stifling routine and convenience of living with my family in Kuwait. Having someone close by to Syria in case my extended family needed anything was also part of the plan.

My parents were supportive as usual.

The struggles on the streets had become vicious and erratic. So had the discussions. Should we compromise? Have we gone too far? What is change? Is this the real deal or a nefarious conspiracy?

Despite all the confusion arising from the fog of rebellion, it seemed crystal clear to me that the repressive regimes—backed by the U.S. or Russia or both or whomever—all had to go. Egypt or Bahrain, Saudi or Iran, Yemen or Syria. No exceptions.

Not everyone shared that sentiment. Especially when it came to Syria.

You guys have it good with Bashar Assad. Fuck corrupt Arab governments and their subservience to imperialism and colonialism. Assad is protecting the country. It's amazing.

Sure... Syria is slightly different from the others. But Assad is not actually fighting imperialism.

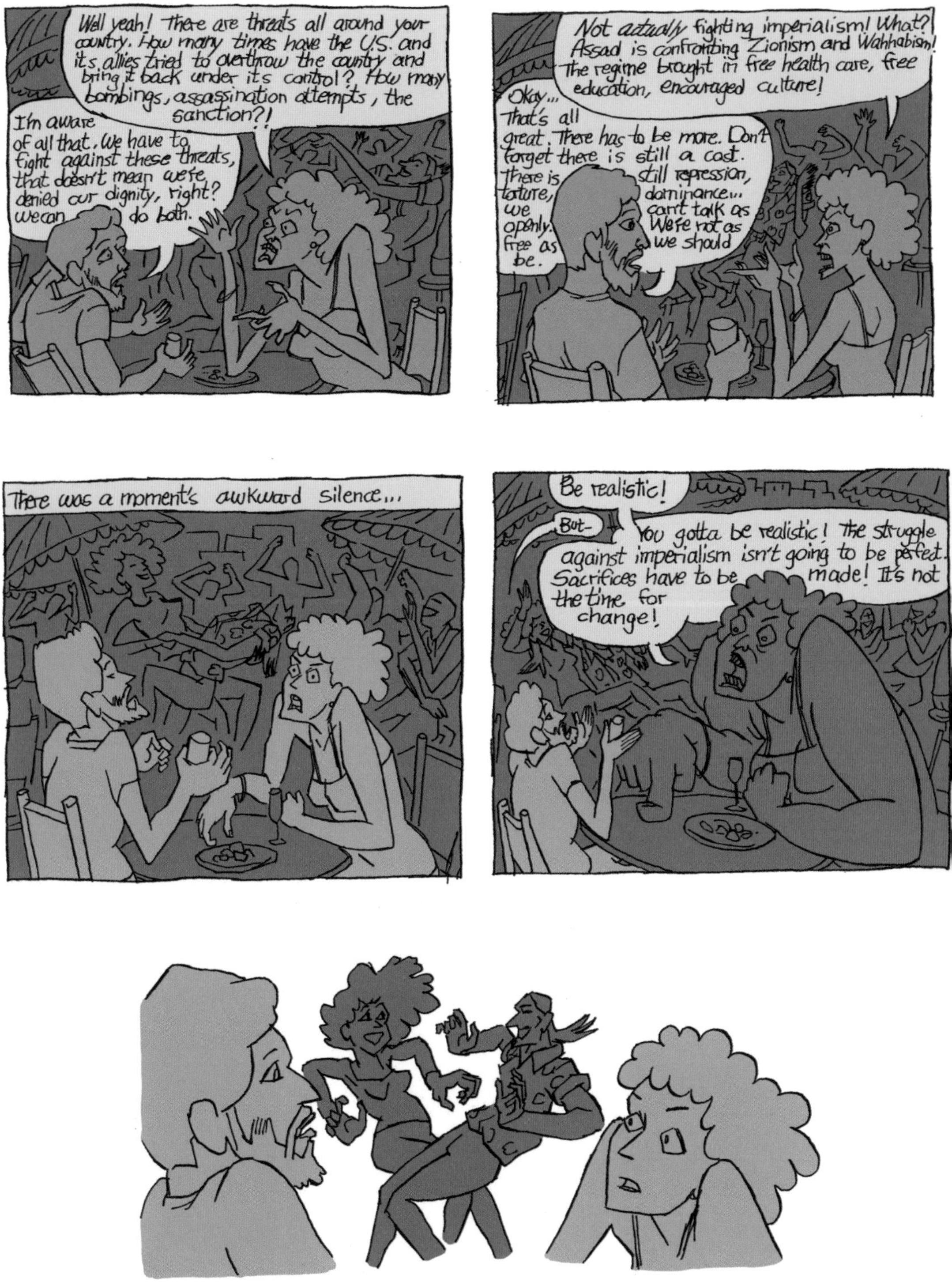
Well yeah! There are threats all around your country. How many times have the U.S. and its allies tried to overthrow the country and bring it back under its control?, How many bombings, assassination attempts, the sanction?!
I'm aware of all that. We have to fight against these threats, that doesn't mean we're denied our dignity, right? We can do both.
Not actually fighting imperialism! What? Assad is confronting Zionism and Wahhabism! The regime brought in free health care, free education, encouraged culture!
Okay... That's all great. There has to be more. Don't forget there is still a cost. There is still repression, torture, dominance... we can't talk as openly. We're not as free as we should be.
There was a moment's awkward silence...
Be realistic!
But-
You gotta be realistic! The struggle against imperialism isn't going to be perfect. Sacrifices have to be made! It's not the time for change!

Do you, I, and we have it good? Is it either a choice between the dictator or the emperor?

Why not refuse both? Where are we? Where are we heading towards? When is it "the right time" for change? Who decides this shit?

Who penned this joke?

Can we make a new one?

Or is this as good as it gets?

11.
RUBBLE IS UNIVERSAL

Yazan Al-Saadi and Ghadi Ghosn

I went to Yemen in the fall of 2016, when I was with Doctors Without Borders (MSF). People tend not to agree on the start date of the war in Yemen. Some will tell you it started when the Saudi-led coalition launched its attack in March 2015; others will argue that it was a year prior, when the Houthis seized control of much of the country; still others will point to the Yemeni uprising in 2011 or even further back to the early 1990s, when then-dictator Ali Abdullah Saleh took control, forcibly unified Yemen, and deepened ties with the West, despite being ruthless to Yemenis. Ali Abdullah Saleh would be ousted in 2012. He would ally with the Houthis during the war with Saudi Arabia and would later be killed by the Houthis in December 2017.

The Saudi-led coalition, which was armed and backed by the United States and the United Kingdom, was very brutal. They instituted a blockade that accelerated famine in Yemen and further pushed an already poor community into deeper poverty. The Houthis, for their part, were also brutal, launching various mini-sieges against cities and towns that opposed them. The country had foreign occupying forces, a secessionist movement in the south, and fundamentalist groups like Al-Qaeda that were all bickering and fighting with one another. The will of the people was ignored.

The toll on Yemen is sobering: nearly 400,000 killed from the violence, at least 85,000 Yemeni children starved to death, and more than 4,000 dead from cholera and other epidemics. Hospitals, homes, cultural sites, and other civilian infrastructure were destroyed, and other war crimes were recorded by various humanitarian and international organizations.

The art for this comic is by Ghadi Ghosn, one of my go-to collaborators.

Page 108 (top): After receiving approval from Saudi and Houthi officials to enter Yemen, I took a small UN propeller plane to Sana'a International Airport, where I was picked up by an MSF driver.

Page 110: First I toured the various sites of air strikes by the Saudi-led coalition. It was very clear on the ground that the attackers were indiscriminate and often hit schools, cultural sites, and other nonmilitary sites.

Page 111: The thumps of air strikes and fighting were a regular feature at night.

Pages 112 (bottom)–114: While touring three hospitals with a Yemeni doctor, I witnessed medical cases that ranged from burns and lost limbs from air strikes to chronic disease, malnutrition, and starvation.

Page 115 (top left): The conversation with the doctor was poignant. Here was a man who had done so much for his community and still felt it wasn't enough.

WELCOME to SANA'A

Jordan
Iraq
Iran
Saudi Arabia
United Arab Emirates
Oman
Yemen
Sudan
Sanáa

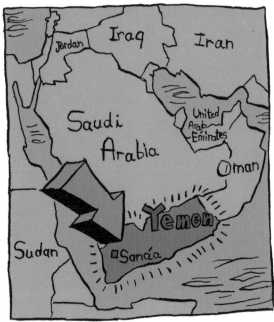

I was in Yemen – mainly in Sana'a – for more than two weeks between October and November to provide communications support for Médecins sans Frontières (MSF, or Doctors Without Borders) teams.

I was a nest of contradictory emotions. Scared as shit, but excited. Nervous, but oddly calm. Contradiction after contradiction.

Yemen was alluring for me in many ways. As a Syrian, with a Canadian passport, my name was Yemeni in Origin. My interest in Yemen peaked during the 2011 Arab uprisings, when they attempted to topple their dictator. I never expected I was going to step foot in the country.

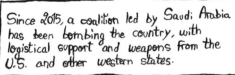

Since 2015, a coalition led by Saudi Arabia has been bombing the country, with logistical support and weapons from the U.S. and other western states.

Let us begin the Sana'a tour of airstrikes.

In Yemen, from March 2015 through September 2016 alone, MSF treated 51,048 victims of war and violence.

There's one.

There's another.

There's another airstrike.

Next to that school.

These sights are familiar to me. I've seen them in places like Syria, Palestine, Lebanon, Iraq.

The universality of rubble ties everything together in a strange way.

Night. I was speaking on the phone with someone I was in love with, safely thousands of miles away.

All of a sudden —

It sounded like the deep rumble of thunder. Man-made thunder.

Wait.

I think there was an airstrike.

Let me hear if there's going to be another one.

Slow seconds pass. My palms moist, my throat dry. I waited.

Nothing. Thankfully.

So yeah, what were we saying?

I am humbled by anyone who can maintain composure under the bombs. I can stand it for a few moments, but constantly?
No fucking way.

I go on a whirlwind tour of the three hospitals that MSF supports: Al-Kuwait University Hospital, Al-Thawra and Al-Joumhouri. The plan is to visit patients and speak with medical staff.

BRAAP, BRAAAP!!

WATCH OUT

Braap, Braap, INCOMING! BRAAP, BRAAP

One patient is a war-wounded man who just underwent surgery to remove a bullet. He's lost under a spell of drugs, reliving a battle.

WOOHOO! Watch OUT!! HAHAHA

BRAAP, BRAAP

INCOMING !! BRAP, BRAAP,

WOOHOO! HAHAHA

At that moment, I felt great sadness for the pawns on the chessboard. They can't even escape their dreams.

This patient is a younger farmer from Abs who survived an airstrike. They thought he was dead when they brought him in, all black and red.

Many surgeries later, we think he can return to a relatively normal life.

that is the hope.

I find myself struggling to look at him as normally as possible. I try a smile. He doesn't pay attention.

I guess he wishes he was back at those fields. I would too.

This patient is a victim of torture.

you are a brave mama and amazing.

He was dumped at the hospital after his torturers discovered that he has AIDS. He lies in bed, a shattered human being.

Some of his friends and his mother are by his side. She loves her son and doesn't understand why the world has treated him so harshly. She is in disbelief over the fact that her husband doesn't want their son to come back home.

Thank you, doctor. You are a godsend for helping my son.

It goes on and on. Patient after patient. Story after tragic fucking story. And more come in every day.

It haunts me too. All those inside Yemen and beyond that we can't help or hear.

No pity in our exchange, refreshingly so; only the camaraderie of misery. There is solidarity even in another's state of hell. It feels powerful and hopeful.

12.
MY HEART BURNS

Yazan Al-Saadi and Tracy Chahwan

Lebanon hosts the greatest number of refugees per capita and per square kilometer in the world. And it also has some of the worst conditions for refugees. There have been around 1.5 million Syrian refugees in Lebanon since 2011; around 200,000 Palestinian refugees since 1948; and around 20,000 other refugees, such as Somalis, Sudanese, Iraqis, and others. One in four people in Lebanon is a refugee. In a state that lacks the appropriate infrastructure to care for refugees, not to mention individuals in power who are interested in doing so, those who seek to exploit the vulnerable have a great advantage.

Tracy Chahwan is the talented artist for this one. She is one of the coolest artists on the Lebanese comics landscape and one of the new generation currently in charge of Samandal.

Page 118 (middle): Established in 1949 in Beirut, Lebanon, as a temporary shelter for Palestinians until they could return home, Shatila is one of twelve refugee camps in the country. Because Israel denies Palestinians the inalienable right of return, they have remained trapped in these camps. To further complicate their situation, Palestinians are denied the ability to work in Lebanon and are caged in what are practically small open-air prisons. Shatila is no longer a Palestinian refugee camp but is instead a camp for the poor. The majority of those sheltering there now are from Syria; the rest are Palestinians, other refugees, South Asian and African workers, and other vulnerable communities.

Page 119 (bottom middle): The core factor underlying xenophobia in Lebanon (beyond the superficiality of sect or nationality) is class.

Page 122 (bottom left): It was hard to witness someone being consumed by guilt because there was no culprit to blame. I tried to convince her that it absolutely wasn't her fault, but I doubt she heard me.

Page 124 (bottom right): My answer to the question of "Who protects the refugees?" is that it must be the refugees themselves. There should be a transnational political body composed of refugees working for the rights of refugees.

Page 127: As we go from the grounded story to the philosophical considerations at the end of this comic, note how Tracy subverts political iconographies here to buttress the universal points being made. And that's because being stateless is something that could happen to every one of us. It's something we should all be concerned about.

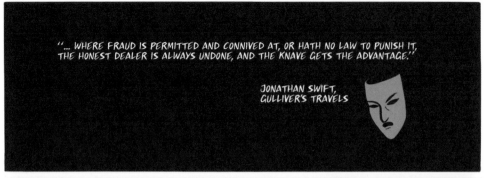

"... WHERE FRAUD IS PERMITTED AND CONNIVED AT, OR HATH NO LAW TO PUNISH IT, THE HONEST DEALER IS ALWAYS UNDONE, AND THE KNAVE GETS THE ADVANTAGE."

JONATHAN SWIFT,
GULLIVER'S TRAVELS

IN THE SUMMER OF *2017*, I WAS IN SHATILA - ONE OF THE WORLD'S OLDEST REFUGEE CAMPS - LOCATED 4.4 KILOMETERS (2.7 MILES) SOUTH FROM BEIRUT'S OPULENT AND EXCLUSIONARY DOWNTOWN.

I WAS COLLECTING TESTIMONIES FROM REFUGEES AND RESIDENTS.

EACH STORY I ENCOUNTERED WAS FILLED WITH FRUSTRATION AND SADNESS.

THE NARRATORS ACHED AND HOPED...

...OR WERE FATALISTIC AND DISMAL TOWARDS THEIR LIVES.

OUT OF ALL THE STORIES THAT DAY, ONE STOOD OUT.

UMM AHMED'S STORY BEGAN LIKE MANY IN SYRIA: FLEEING THE WAR.

ARRIVING IN LEBANON, SHE AND HER FAMILY MANAGED TO FIND AN AFFORDABLE APARTMENT IN BEIRUT'S OUTSKIRTS. NOT WHAT THEY'D BEEN USED TO, BUT NO WAR HERE.

UNSURE WHEN THEY'D RETURN TO SYRIA, THEY TRIED TO REBUILD A SEMBLANCE OF THEIR PAST LIVES.

BUT LEBANON IS VERY EXPENSIVE. AID AND UNSKILLED WORK BARELY KEPT THEM AFLOAT. IT WAS RISKY, SINCE SYRIAN REFUGEES ARE RESTRICTED FROM WORK IN LEBANON.

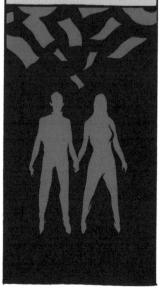

HOSTILITY FROM POLITICIANS, MILITARY, AND NATIONAL AND INTERNATIONAL MEDIA TOWARDS REFUGEES INFLAMED XENOPHOBIA AND RESTRICTIONS INCREASED.

UMM AHMED AND HER FAMILY OFTEN CONFINED THEMSELVES TO THEIR APARTMENT.

ALIENATION, ISOLATION, FRUSTRATION, AND FEAR DOMINATED.

LIFE IN LEBANON CLEARLY WASN'T VIABLE. LIKE MANY OTHERS, THEY CONSIDERED EUROPE. IT WASN'T EASY TO GET THERE AND LEGAL RESETTLEMENT WASN'T GUARANTEED. IT COULD TAKE MONTHS OR YEARS IF IT HAPPENED AT ALL.

AND SMUGGLERS POSED THEIR OWN, POTENTIALLY FATAL, DANGERS.

WHAT TO DO?

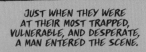

JUST WHEN THEY WERE AT THEIR MOST TRAPPED, VULNERABLE, AND DESPERATE, A MAN ENTERED THE SCENE.

FLASHING ID FROM THE UNITED NATIONS REFUGEE AGENCY (UNRWA), HE SAID...

I PROMISE SALVATION: A PLANE TO EUROPE! IT'LL COST THOUSANDS OF DOLLARS, BUT I'LL TAKE CARE OF ALL THE PAPERWORK. ALL YOU HAVE TO DO IS WAIT AND GET ON THAT PLANE.

THIS, I ASSURE YOU, IS YOUR BEST CHANCE!

AND SO UMM AHMED AND HER FAMILY PASSED ALONG THEIR DOCUMENTS, AND THEY PAID THE MAN MONEY FROM WHAT REMAINED FROM THEIR SAVINGS AND FROM THE BELONGINGS THEY SOLD.

AS PROMISED, AT AN AGREED TIME AT NIGHT, TRANSPORTATION ARRIVED IN FRONT OF THEIR APARTMENT. UMM AHMED, WITH HER FAMILY, AND AROUND 30 OTHER FAMILIES WERE WHISKED AWAY TO THE AIRPORT.

THEY WERE DROPPED OFF AND TOLD TO WAIT, THE PLANE WAS BEING PREPARED.

SO THEY WAITED; EAGER, ANXIOUS, AND HOPEFUL. THEY WAITED, AND WAITED SOME MORE.

FINALLY, TO THEIR HORROR, OFFICIALS CAME OVER TO DEMAND THEY STOP LOITERING AND LEAVE THE AIRPORT.

THERE WAS NO PLANE. NO JOURNEY TO EUROPE. IT HAD ALL BEEN AN ELABORATE SCAM.

BROKE, FINANCIALLY AND EMOTIONALLY, THEY RETURNED TO THEIR BARREN APARTMENT.

UMM AHMED REACHED OUT TO UNHCR, BUT WAS TOLD THE MAN SHE WAS LOOKING FOR WASN'T EMPLOYED THERE.

THEN THE PHONE CALLS STARTED. IF THEY CONTINUE WITH QUESTIONS, LIVES WILL BE IN DANGER. YOUNG LIVES.

THERE SHE WAS IN THAT SMALL ROOM, RAW EMOTION POURING OUT, HEART BITTER. HER WORDS WERE LIKE HER THOUGHTS—ENSNARED IN A LOOP.

MY HEART BURNS.
THIS ISN'T OUR FAULT, RIGHT?
MY HUSBAND IS BROKEN AS A MAN BECAUSE OF THIS.
HE SLEEPS AND DOESN'T MOVE ANYMORE.
WE HAVE NOTHING.
THEY DESTROYED US.
MY GOD. WE ARE GOOD PEOPLE, WE'VE NOT HARMED ANYONE.

WHY DID THIS HAPPEN? WHAT DO WE DO? WHO CAN I TURN TO? THE POLICE? NO! UNHCR?

TRAUMATIZED, LOST, HURT, FURIOUS, OBSESSIVELY AND DESPERATELY TRYING TO UNDERSTAND THE HOWS AND WHYS OF IT ALL.

THEY'LL BLAME US FOR TRYING TO LEAVE FOR EUROPE! HOW COULD THIS HAPPEN? WHAT DO I DO? WHERE IS JUSTICE? THEY SAID THEY'D GO AFTER THE CHILDREN! OH GOD! HOW COULD A HUMAN DO THIS TO OTHERS? MY HEART...IT BURNS SO MUCH!

FUCK. THAT. GUY.

YEARS LATER, WORKING ON THIS COMIC, I CORRESPONDED WITH LISA ABOU KHALED, UNHCR'S PUBLIC INFORMATION OFFICER IN BEIRUT.

UNHCR has received reports of individuals and/or organizations claiming to provide support for resettlement, mainly by helping refugees in filling forms from the various Embassies. Such initiatives and activities are not necessarily always fraudulent, as the forms can be legitimate forms from the Embassies. However, indeed, UNHCR is regularly informed of fraudulent activities that promise refugees various levels of support.

THERE ARE NO COHESIVE LAWS FOR REFUGEES THAT ALLOW FOR SAFE, LEGAL, QUICK MEANS FOR RESETTLEMENT, ESPECIALLY ON A MASS SCALE.

WHAT EXISTS IS A MASSIVE AND TANGLED BUREAUCRATIC WEB, STRETCHING ACROSS BORDERS, EVER CHANGING, OFTEN FOR THE WORSE.

INTO THAT VOID COMES OPPORTUNITY FOR EXPLOITATION AND PROFIT.

I SPOKE WITH HUMAN RIGHTS LAWYER DIALA CHEHADE.

WHAT DRIVES THESE SCAMS AND ABUSES?

TALKS ON RETURNING REFUGEES, NO SAFETY GUARANTEES BY THE SYRIAN REGIME, AND A HISTORY OF HOSTILITY AND LEGAL RESTRICTIONS IN LEBANON AGAINST 'FOREIGNERS', SO PEOPLE BREAK THE LAW TO LIVE.

ARE JUDGES AND SECURITY FORCES PART OF THE PROBLEM?

IT'S A MIXED BAG. YOU HEAR SOME GOOD STORIES... AND SOME HORRIBLE ONES.

SO WHO PROTECTS THE REFUGEES?

THIS ISN'T UNIQUE TO LEBANON. RESEARCH AND REPORTS FROM OTHER COUNTRIES HAVE SHOWN SIMILAR PATTERNS AND GAPS THAT ALLOW FRAUD TO FLOURISH AGAINST REFUGEES.

A LOCAL NGO IN JORDAN CALLED THE LEGAL ASSISTANCE UNIT OF THE ARAB RENAISSANCE FOR DEMOCRACY AND DEVELOPMENT (ARDD) OBSERVED THAT MOST FRAUD AGAINST SYRIAN REFUGEES IS RELATED TO RESETTLEMENT OR ILLEGAL MIGRATION, WITH AROUND 70% OF THE CASES INVOLVING PROMISES OF THE LATTER.

ARDD REPORTED THAT INDIVIDUALS OFTEN POSE AS UNHCR STAFF, STAFF OF WESTERN EMBASSIES, FAKE VISA/MIGRATION COMPANIES, OR LICENSING COMPANIES. THE SCHEMES ARE OFTEN ELABORATE.

ARDD WENT ON TO STATE THAT "THE PERPETRATORS' HIGH LEVEL OF ATTENTION TO DETAIL INDICATES THAT THESE WERE NOT ISOLATED CASES, BUT RATHER PART OF A LARGER CRIMINAL NETWORK. BASED ON THE ACCOUNT OF REFUGEES, IT APPEARS THAT A LOT OF MONEY AND EFFORT IS BEING PUT BEHIND THE COUNTERFEITING OF LOGOS, COPYING UNIFORMS, AND THE USE OF MULTIPLE MOBILE PHONE NUMBERS."

SECONDLY, WHEN REFUGEES ARE VICTIMS, THEY ARE HESITANT TO LOOK FOR LEGAL RECOURSE OR REPORT CASES TO UNHCR BECAUSE THEY FEAR "GETTING IN TROUBLE THEMSELVES FOR TRYING TO DO SOMETHING ILLEGAL" OR "THEY WILL BE NEGATIVELY IMPACTED - EITHER THROUGH LEGAL COMPLICATIONS OR OTHER CONCERNS."

WITHOUT AN APPROACHABLE LEGAL PROCESS THAT OFFERS JUSTICE AND PROTECTION, MOST ORGANIZATIONS HAVE RESORTED TO AWARENESS RAISING CAMPAIGNS. KNOWLEDGE, IT IS HOPED, COULD COUNTER THE CONFUSION, FEAR, AND IGNORANCE THAT SCAMMERS THRIVE IN.

ABOU KHALED TELLS ME THAT UNHCR HAS TAKEN A NUMBER OF STEPS TO RAISE AWARENESS AMONG THE REFUGEE COMMUNITY THROUGH OUTREACH VOLUNTEERS

FACEBOOK PAGES

PARTICIPATION OF UNHCR RESETTLEMENT STAFF IN A RADIO SHOW TO CLARIFY THE PROCEDURE, ETC.

LEAFLETS

THE AWARENESS RAISING CAMPAIGNS HAVE THEIR SUCCESSES, ACCORDING TO BOTH ARDD AND UNHCR. BUT IT CLEARLY DOESN'T HELP THOSE WHO HAVE ALREADY FALLEN INTO A TRAP. NOR DOES IT AIM TO TACKLE THE TRUE HEART OF THE MATTER.

THERE IS A BIGGER SCAM AT WORK HERE, WHICH ALLOWS OTHER SCAMS AGAINST REFUGEES TO THRIVE.

THIS IS THE GRAND SCAM OF ARTIFICIAL NATION-STATES, HARD BORDERS, RISING WALLS, PASSPORT HIERARCHIES AND VISA REGIMES— ALL BUILT ON THE DELUDED NOTIONS OF "PURITY" VS. THE "OTHER" AND OF AN "US" VS. A "THEM."

BUT HUMANS HAVE NEVER NOT BEEN ON THE MOVE, SEARCHING FOR A SAFE PLACE TO LIVE AS NORMALLY AS POSSIBLE, AND TO STRIVE. IT'S ENCODED IN OUR DNA.

HUMANS CAUSE WARS, POVERTY, AND CLIMATE CHANGE. NONE OF THAT IS SLOWING DOWN. IT'S GETTING WORSE. AND BECAUSE OF THAT, PEOPLE WILL CONTINUE TO MOVE.

WILL THE BORDERS COME DOWN FOR THE DESPERATE, FLEEING IN SEARCH OF A BETTER LIFE? WILL THERE BE DIGNIFIED AND HUMANE RECEPTION FOR THOSE WHO DO COME IN?

OR WILL THE ADVANTAGE GO TO THE KNAVE, AND WE SIMPLY WATCH THIS DANCE AGAIN AND AGAIN?

13.
UNSTOPPABLE FORCE

Yazan Al-Saadi and Omar Khouri

This was a challenging comic to make. We were commissioned to create a comic showing the impact of the COVID-19 pandemic on the financial and economic crisis in Lebanon, which was by all accounts one of the worst financial crises of recent times. That was already a sizeable charge.

Then tragedy struck the Port of Beirut on August 4, 2020. It also meant another macabre record for Lebanon. A large amount of ammonium nitrate (around 2,750 tonnes, or the equivalent of about 1.1 kilotons of TNT), which had been haphazardly stored in a warehouse, exploded, killing more than 250 people, injuring more than 7,000, and leaving around 300,000 homeless. This was considered one of the most powerful nonnuclear explosions in human history.

Many state actors of various political persuasions were behind the explosion. And yet, to date, not one important person has been held to account for this crime. The state has tried to move on. But the victims and their families still feel a great deal of rage toward the government's handling of this incident.

For this comic, Omar Khouri was once again my collaborator, and here he embraced a completely different style.

Page 131: This was not an easy page for Khouri to draw, as he had to review video footage of the explosion multiple times in order to draw it accurately. This was understandably traumatizing.

Page 132 (top): The choice of incorporating a Chinese proverb in a story about Lebanon may seem out of place. I felt it was fitting because I wanted to make a larger point about how the proverbial stories we often tell ourselves have broad, if not universal, appeal.

Page 132 (bottom right): The boat on its side is drawn from an aerial photograph of one of the boats that sank after the blast.

Page 135 (middle): A women's rights protest had to be called off when the pandemic struck. In the next few panels I note how the pandemic was a godsend for those in power.

Page 137 (top left): The lira in June 2020 was valued at over 9,000 Lebanese lira to one US dollar. Now, in 2024, one US dollar is valued at 89,000 Lebanese lira.

Page 137 (top right): When I wrote this comic, more than half of the Lebanese population was living in poverty. Now, in 2024, an estimated 80 percent of the Lebanese population lives in poverty.

Page 139 (middle): A new government was formed after elections were held in 2022. Nothing substantial has changed to improve the standard of living in Lebanon.

UN STOP PABLE FORCE:

the pandemic explodes in Lebanon

By:
Yazan al-Saadi
and Omar Khouri

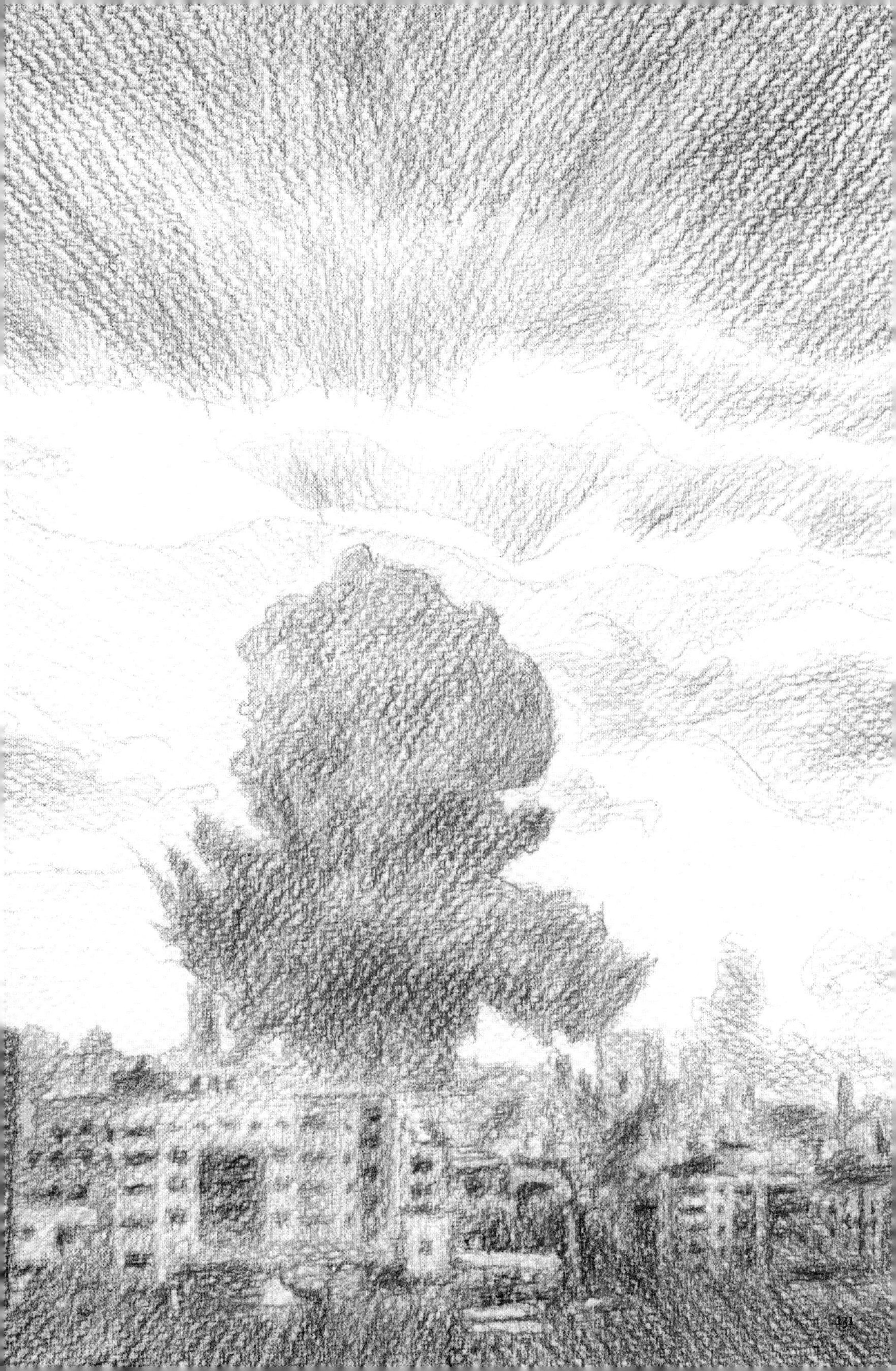

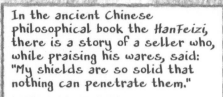

In the ancient Chinese philosophical book the *HanFeizi*, there is a story of a seller who, while praising his wares, said: "My shields are so solid that nothing can penetrate them."

The seller added, "My spears are so sharp that they can penetrate anything."

On Nov. 21, 2013, a cargo ship carrying 2,750 tons of ammonium nitrate arrived in Beirut, but was deemed unfit to travel on by port authorities. The crew were forced to wait on their decrepit ship.

Occasional reports were issued about the danger the nitrate posed so close to the city. The last report was sent on July 20, 2020, and the prime minister and president were CC'd. It warned that Beirut could be blown up.

In October 2014, the ship was impounded and the crew allowed to go home. Lebanese port authorities stacked the bags of nitrate haphazardly in a warehouse.

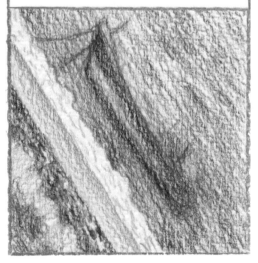

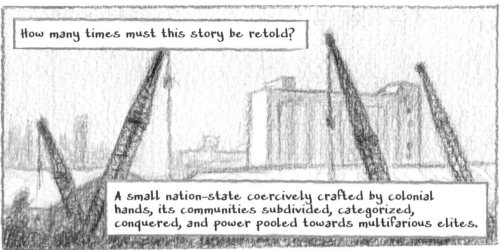

How many times must this story be retold?

A small nation-state coercively crafted by colonial hands, its communities subdivided, categorized, conquered, and power pooled towards multifarious elites.

Vying for a bigger slice of power, the elites fight, and the country burns for 15 years.

Eventually, they conclude that peace is more prosperous than feuds.

And they collectively gorge themselves on extracted profit. Garbage and despair fill the streets...

Hearing the seller's words, someone asked, "What happens when your spear meets your shield?"

To this question, the seller could give no reply.

Communities in Lebanon refused to submit.
Cycles of protest have marked the past 20 years.

Born of discontent against brutal
systems, a spear is flung.

Yet each time, the protests fail
to achieve meaningful change.
The spear falls short.

But quickly others come
and pick it up, pausing
only to sharpen its point.

Ahead, a shield:
the state, the system.
Forged by these
warlords-cum-
politicians, dinky
despots lording over
their patriarchal
fiefdoms.

Its strength is
bolstered by the
shifting gravities of
regional rivalries
and superpowered
psychotic nations
at play.

The Lebanese
government has
dissolved in the
face of protest
before, only to
reform again
with superficial
changes by the
same power
brokers' edicts.

In Jan. 2020, a new government of "experts" was appointed. Fresh faces to mask the rotten body.

The shield seemed impenetrable.

Yet, the spear flew on. Twice this spring Parliament was besieged; rocks and fireworks matched tear gas and bullets.

The spear felt unstoppable.

Then history, and the world, swerved. Separate from the pitched struggle between state and people, and owing allegiance to none, came the pandemic. On March 15, a nationwide lockdown began.

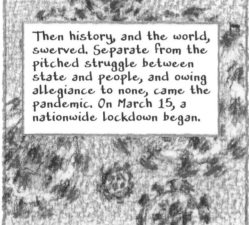

Protests require bodies on the streets, while pandemic necessitates isolation.

The lockdown's early days were filled with terror and anxiety.

Thus the shield had the advantage: Common sense measures must be followed for public health.

Gripped by fear and uncertainty, the streets were forced to be still.

With glee, the state unleashed curfews, court cases against protesters, further cuts to essential services like electricity, and more restrictions on bank accounts.

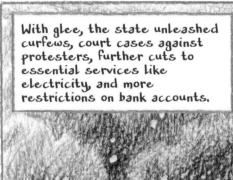

A dash of torture by Lebanese security forces and political party thugs, too.

For those in need, the state did little. It announced a one-time cash donation of $140 for a limited number of families, then postponed it indefinitely.

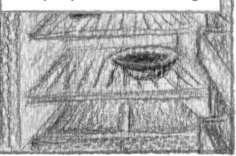

Meanwhile, food rotted in warm fridges and generator fumes filled nostrils.

Vicious anger was caged indoors, while suicide claimed the streets.

By June, the Lebanese economy plunged into a death spiral.

Political bickering and decades-old patterns of exploitation and theft, coupled with the increasing weight of a pandemic, finally bankrupted the country.

As "normality" cracked apart, protests reappeared... sheer spite seemed to keep the spear afloat.

By mid-June, the Lebanese lira devalued by more than 80%, third in global hyperinflation, behind Venezuela and Zimbabwe and just ahead of Syria. People's savings and earnings instantly vanished.

Now, over half the Lebanese population live in poverty, which could easily rise to 75%. Lebanon hosts millions of refugees and migrant workers. Their already destabilized lives have become more grim.

In July, the pandemic bit deeply, and the authorities floundered. Infection rates skyrocketed, and overworked, underpaid hospital staff relied on dwindling supplies.

Businesses closed, and food prices soared more. People planned to flee the country.

Then came August, and calamity.

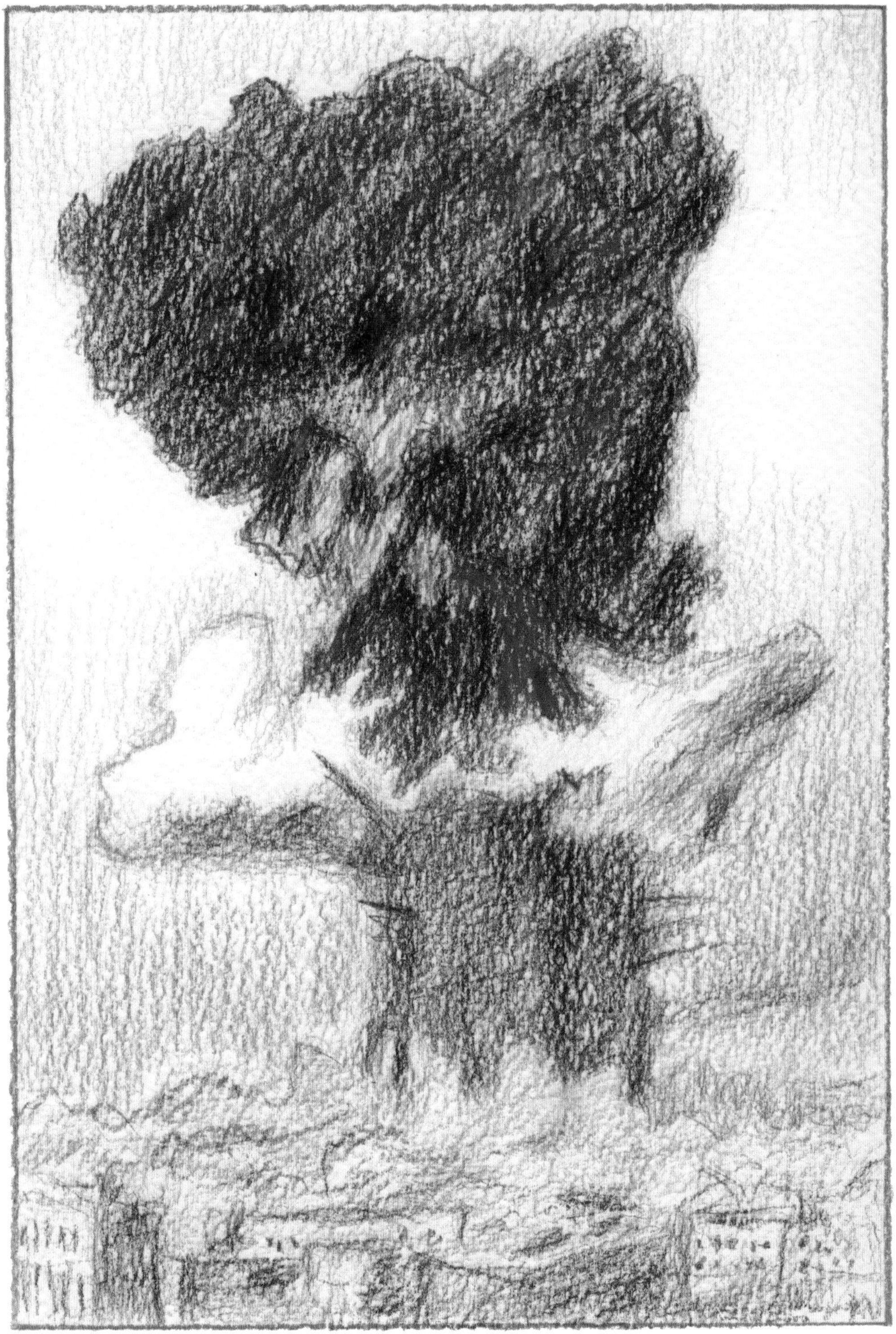

The hundreds who perished and the thousands injured in the Beirut blast of August 4, 2020, were of diverse identities, ages, nationalities, hopes, dreams, classes, and creeds.

Months have now passed, and official investigations haven't released any conclusions nor made substantial arrests.

The pandemic and explosion are harbingers. They bid us beware the shield's future; it's a dead end.

Already the government has fallen and been served up again as a new order of recycled faces. It is now a centennial since "Greater Lebanon" was first forcibly founded.

Fury and rage have refilled the streets. The spear still approaches.

Impact is inevitable.

Tomorrow, a year, a decade, a generation from now? I do not know.

But hear and be certain, for I have nothing to sell.

At closing curtain, the spear must pierce the shield, or brace for death's knell.

14.
WHOSE LIVES MATTER: DEATH IN THE PERIPHERY

Yazan Al-Saadi and Ghadi Ghosn

Whose lives matter? A worldwide hierarchy of value presupposes that if one has a certain skin color or degree of wealth, their life (and death) has more worth than others. I grapple with this idea when thinking of certain events in my own life, like growing up in Kuwait after the First Gulf War, and then 9/11 and the war on Afghanistan and Iraq, and so many other tragedies. We know that, in reality, not all lives matter. But we also know that it doesn't have to be this way.

Ghadi Ghosn handled the art for this dispatch.

Page 143 (top and middle): I am still haunted by this poor bird.

Page 144 (top): After Kuwait's liberation from the brutal occupation by the Iraqis, we were dealt a lot of propaganda in school, some of which was based on fact.

Page 144 (middle left): In the "Highway of Death" incident, US-led coalition forces ruthlessly killed hundreds of Iraqi soldiers retreating from Kuwait, along with civilians of various nationalities. The horror is seared into our minds.

Page 144 (bottom left): In an interview with Lesley Stahl on the American television newsmagazine *60 Minutes* (May 12, 1996), Madeleine Albright, then US ambassador to the United Nations, stated that the death of more than half a million children in Iraq under the embargo was "worth it."

Page 145 (top): According to a report issued in May 2023 by the Watson Institute for International and Public Affairs at Brown University, the United States' "global war on terror" resulted in an estimated total of 4.5 to 4.7 million direct and indirect deaths.

Page 146 (bottom left): The battle of Arsal took place in August 2014 in a Lebanese town near the Syrian border. Fundamentalist armed groups, including the Syrian jihadist group Al-Nusra Front, attacked Lebanese forces in an attempt to take control of the town. Other than the soldiers who died in combat, around fifty civilians were killed and four hundred wounded.

Page 147 (top right): The tit-for-tat between Israel and Iran raises important concerns about a potential nuclear conflict between the two. The best and only solution is a denuclearized zone imposed on the entire region and on everyone.

WHOSE LIVES MATTER?

DEATH IN THE PERIPHERY

WRITTEN BY YAZAN AL-SAADI
ILLUSTRATED BY GHADI GHOSN

I first met death accidentally when I was around three or four years old.

I was holding a small bird in my hands. It was an exciting moment.
Too exciting.

And I held this tiny fragile bird too tightly.

So it died.

Why is this bird not moving?
Why did it feel lighter?
Will anyone miss this bird?

What did I do?

I didn't and couldn't understand.

The older I got, the more familiar I became with a particular fact about death:

The darker your skin color, the poorer and further away from the metropole you are, the less value your death has.

I went to elementary school in Kuwait. After the First Gulf War, we were taught about the deaths and executions that had occurred.

I still remember scenes from a video shown to us of Kuwaitis being hung and shot in a public square by Iraqi authorities.

The lesson was clear: look at this evil.

At the same time, I also saw images of the infamous "Highway of Death", in which hundreds of Iraqi soldiers and civilians were slaughtered during a retreat back to Iraq.

No talk of evil here. They deserved being burnt to ash. These bodies were looters, rapists, criminals. Don't waste your tears.

The war was followed by sanctions on Iraq throughout the 1990s, slowly killing off over a million Iraqis (500,000 of which were children) across the border from where I lived.

I felt a weird cognitive dissonance.

The price was worth it.

Wasn't this evil too?

Madeleine Albright

The second uprising in Palestine in 2000 left thousands dead and was met with a shrug internationally. The world's strong reaction to 9/11 a year later forced a realization on me...

...Not even death could escape life's inequalities.

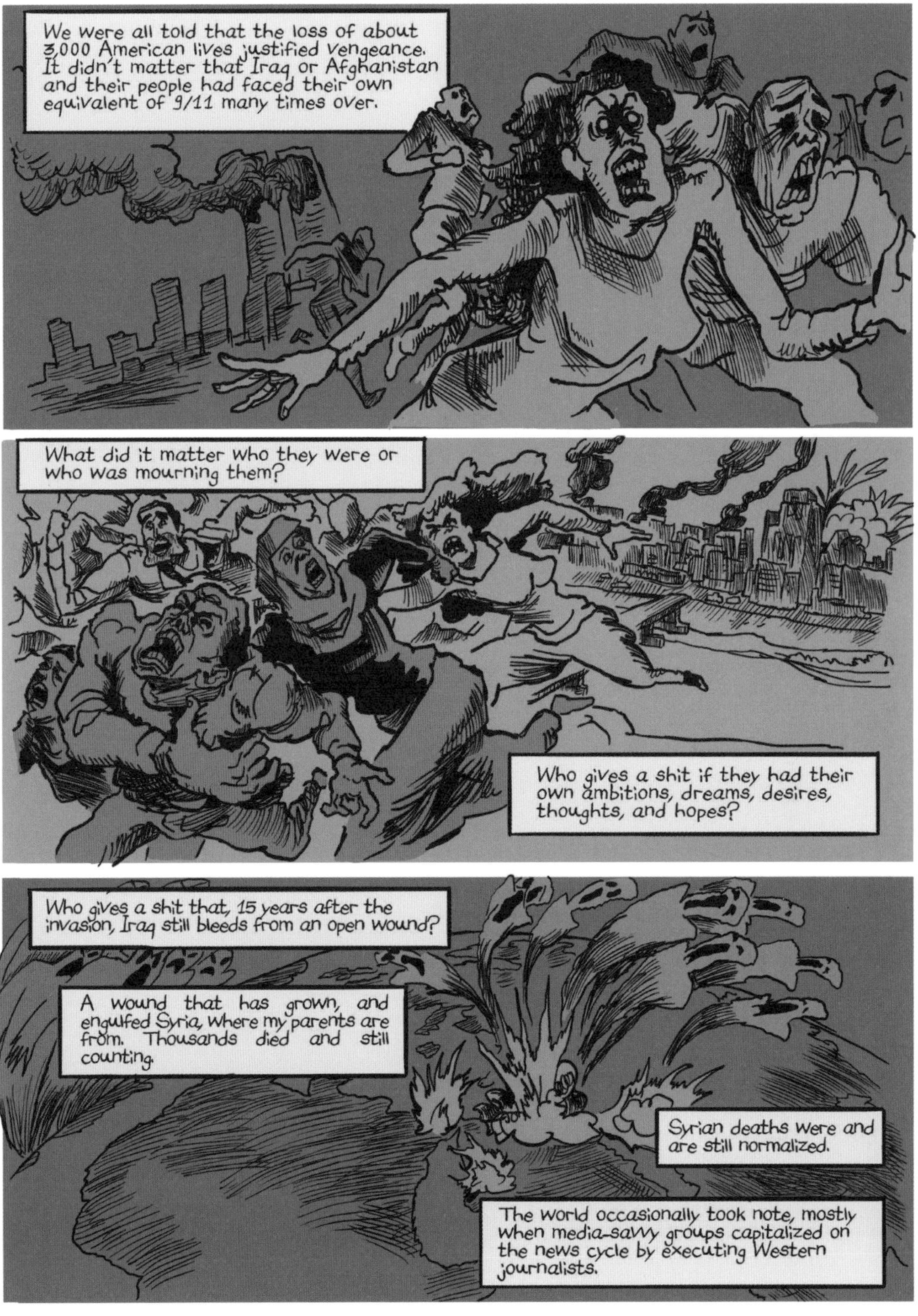
We were all told that the loss of about 3,000 American lives justified vengeance. It didn't matter that Iraq or Afghanistan and their people had faced their own equivalent of 9/11 many times over.
What did it matter who they were or who was mourning them?
Who gives a shit if they had their own ambitions, dreams, desires, thoughts, and hopes?
Who gives a shit that, 15 years after the invasion, Iraq still bleeds from an open wound?
A wound that has grown, and engulfed Syria, where my parents are from. Thousands died and still counting.
Syrian deaths were and are still normalized.
The world occasionally took note, mostly when media-savvy groups capitalized on the news cycle by executing Western journalists.

I was a journalist myself by then, working in Beirut. The question of mourning came up often.

From 2013-2016, there were bombings in Beirut and other towns in Lebanon by armed groups linked to the Syrian civil war.

Over 180 lives were snuffed out.

The questions repeated on angry lips in the Lebanese capital. Why were our deaths not mourned like those in Paris, Belgium, and Boston? Where was our Je suis?

Do our lives not matter?

There was some irony to this.

Because that question was also asked by people in the Lebanese border town of Arsal, where ferocious battles were taking place between the Lebanese military and armed groups spilling over from the neighboring Syrian Civil War.

Hundreds of civilians were caught in the cross-fire and destruction.

The communities of Arsal asked "Who mourns us? Do we not matter too?"

But Beirut just seemed to churn along, blind and aloof about their fate.

It's May 2018, and I now work for an international medical humanitarian organization that operates in war zones. I'm at home in Beirut, writing this comic.

My mind is distracted by the news.

Talk is growing again of a regional war between Israel and Iran, which would inevitably include Lebanon.

And I really wonder if destruction and death are truly ahead...

Will I be a footnote, statistic, collateral, or an unfortunate circumstance?

Is my death—and others' potential deaths—worth it?

And who will mourn us then?

"Good God, how can you kill someone and then take even his own death away from him?"
—Kamel Daoud,
-The Meursault Investigation-

ABOUT THE ARTISTS

Tracy Chahwan is a comic book artist and illustrator. Her first graphic novel, *Beirut Bloody Beirut*, tells the story of two girls lost in Beirut at night. She has worked on multiple short comics also marked by dark humor and chaotic urban experiences. Her illustration work focuses mainly on music visuals for record labels and underground music collectives. She currently lives in Pennsylvania in the United States.

Ganzeer writes, draws, paints, and designs stuff. His stories have been published in prestigious anthologies such as *Who Will Speak for America?* and *The Big Book of Cyberpunk*. His art has been exhibited in galleries and museums such as The Brooklyn Museum in New York, The Palace of the Arts in Cairo, and the V&A in London. His serialized graphic novel *The Solar Grid* garnered him The MoCCA Award for Excellence and a Global Thinker Award from *Foreign Policy*.

Ghadi Ghosn was born in 1984 in Lebanon. He studied illustration at ALBA (Académie Libanaise des Beaux-Arts) and is renowned for his comics, drawings, and illustrations. He works as a freelancer and is currently working on his first graphic novel in France.

Omar Khouri is a cofounder of the *Samandal Comics* magazine, the first experimental comics periodical in the Arab world. In 2010, his sociopolitical comic strip "Utopia" won best Arabic Comic at the International Comic Book Festival of Algeria (F.I.B.D.A). He currently lives and works in North Lebanon.

Sirène Moukheiber is an illustrator and comics artist. She previously worked as an illustrator and art director with AJ+ in Doha, Qatar, and is currently a visual content creator with the WHRDMENA coalition.

Hicham Rahma is passionate about drawing and art. He has worked nearly two decades in a career as a designer and art director on branding, package design, and print illustration, all while continuing to draw and paint. He is a cofounder of *TOKTOK*, an award-winning comics magazine in Egypt, and has received national and international awards for his book cover designs.

Enas Satir is a Sudanese visual artist currently living in Toronto. Her art focuses on cultural projects revolving around blackness, politics, and feminism. Most of her art is inspired by the complexity and beauty of her country, Sudan.